German Uniforms of the 20th Century Volume 2
Uniforms of the Infantry
1919-to the Present

UNIFORMS OF THE INFANTRY

1919-TO THE PRESENT

JÖRG M. HORMANN

Schiffer Publishing Ltd.
1469 Morstein Road, West Chester, Pennsylvania 19380

The author is responsible for the contents.

Translated by Dr. Edward Force, Central Connecticut State University

Library of Congress Catalog Number: 89-063362.

Printed in the United States of America.
ISBN: 0-88740-215-1

Originally published under the title, "Uniformen der Infanterie" 1919 bis heute, copyright Podzun-Pallas-Verlag, GmbH, Markt 9, 6360 Friedberg/H.3, © 1989, ISBN: 3-7909-0382-5.

Published by Schiffer Publishing, Ltd.
1469 Morstein Road
West Chester, Pennsylvania 19380
Please write for a free catalog.
This book may be purchased from the publisher.
Please include $2.00 postage.
Try your bookstore first.

Contents

Introduction

In this, the second volume of the **German Uniforms of the 20th Century** series, a subject is treated that does not enjoy very great "popularity", because it brings certain problems with it.

A book about infantry uniforms from 1919 to the present cannot be complete. The largest body of troops in the various German armies, making up more than 60% of them, was and is simply structured only at first glance, in terms of its inner organization. The foot soldiers, as a group, still had their leading position until the end of World War I, and even in World War II they were partially decisive. With the appearance of motorized, wheeled and treaded vehicles as means of transport and fighting in the German army, the role of the infantry also changed slowly from that of troops purely on foot to motorized and, nowadays, armored units.

Moving the troops forward, formerly a time-consuming process, is reduced to a minimum today thanks to full motorization. The actual battle assignment of the infantry has remained that of being placed to go and fight in the country. These troops, when they became motorized, took on a new quality that made itself known even in the nomenclature of the various infantry troop types. Today the infantrymen call themselves pursuit troops or armored grenadiers. In World War II there were still armored fusiliers and ski troops, along with the significant abbreviation "mot." added to the type of troop.

With the exceptions of the mountain soldiers and paratroopers, who will find their places in further volumes of this series, the development of the infantry uniforms will be portrayed here with a multitude of color and black-and-white pictures. Along with the development of the uniform, the infantry decorations of World War II have been given a good deal of space. The photographic material is a special treat for the interested reader. For the most part, it consists of unpublished photographs with excellent detail, which will also please the collector of military memorabilia. The chronological arrangement of the development of the uniform is especially fascinating, since it makes the maintenance of or departure from tradition particularly clear.

For their cooperation and special help, I would like to thank the following gentlemen: Gottfried Ingold, Gerhard Rudloff and Wilhelm G. Steifensand. In addition, I am grateful to the press staff of the Federal Defense Ministry and the Armed Forces Office, Recruiting Section.

Garbsen, Autumn 1989 — Jörg-M. Hormann

Infantry Uniforms in the Weimar Republic

After World War I had ended with the signing of the armistice on November 11, 1918, about two million soldiers of the field army returned to their garrisons with about 100,000 officers. War-weariness and the revolutionary climate in Germany led to disorderly demobilization of almost all the troops, so that in December of 1918 the country's military power consisted of "officers without troops."

In this situation, which was characterized not only by internal unrest but also by military conflicts on the eastern borders of the Reich, bands of volunteers came to the aid of the government. The free corps mainly recruited soldiers of the field army, and their military potential had to be taken into consideration in the formation of the temporary Reichswehr as of March 1919, and the later Reichsheer as of January 1921.

In terms of uniforming, there were several phases: Peacetime army/free corps, temporary Reichswehr, and subsequent Reichsheer. Many uniform parts and the impossibility of a

General of the Infantry Wilhelm Heye, chief of the military command, greets officers of the Reichsheer before 1927. The officers still wear black lacquered leather assault straps on their peaked caps. Per order of July 22, 1927, cap cords, silver for officers and gold for generals, were introduced.

completely new uniforming led to the retention of the proven combat uniforms in use at the end of World War I. To be sure, many changes were made, particularly to the insignia used in the peacetime army and the temporary Reichswehr. Shoulder patches and flaps, as well as the patches of braid worn by non-commissioned officers, fell victim to the revolutionary climate, and the efforts to make the uniforms of all ranks as "equal" as

The subsequent general of the infantry, Erich Wöllwarth, as a major on the general staff around 1915. The combat jacket of the imperial army served as the basis for the combat and dress uniforms of the Reichswehr. Eight buttons, plus the stiff collar and diagonal side pockets, are characteristic of this uniform piece.

According to the temporary decisions of January 19, 1919 regarding clothing and uniforms in the peacetime army, dark blue sleeve stripes on the left upper arm were introduced as insignia of rank. The individual stripes with a width of 1.5 centimeters indicated the non-commissioned officer. Until the time of the temporary Reichswehr, the uniforms and insignia of the free corps could continue to be worn. Here a soldier wears the insignia of the Hessian Free Corps on his collar (HFK on an oak leaf).

possible were clear to see. For the ranks, the introduction of the peaked cap and, since the establishment of the temporary Reichswehr, the guard patches on the collar, were a particular upgrading. Guard patches had been reserved for only the guard units in the imperial army and regarded as a special decoration. As of March 6, 1919 all ranks of the army were given guard patches as insignia for their collars. With the exception of the generality and a short period of service-arm insignia in the Bundeswehr, these double patches on the collar have been worn by all German army soldiers.

Large double braid patches on the collar and shoulder bars were part of the temporary Reichswehr uniform. Insignia of rank on the sleeves cannot be seen here.

The transitional period from peacetime army to temporary Reichswehr: In the back row are two non-commissioned officers with dark blue cloth stripes on their upper arms as insignia of rank. At the right front is a non-commissioned officer of the temporary Reichswehr.

The people involved found out relatively soon that experimenting with new forms of insignia of rank was bound to be unsuccessful. The practical experience and traditional aspects led, in the uniforming of the Reichsheer as of January 1, 1921, to the reintroduction of shoulder patches and flaps to show rank and service arm. In the peacetime army, blue stripes of cloth on the left sleeve were intended to be insignia of rank. The temporary Reichswehr made a similar attempt to use strips of braid, one centimeter wide, on both lower arms for non-commissioned officers and men. This form of indicating ranks, taken from the navy, did not last. Along with the braid stripes, the temporary Reichswehr also used rank-group insignia in the form of

Above: on October 5, 1922 Lieutenant Paul Scheuerpflug of Infantry Regiment 15 in Kassel was married. Until 1927, there was no class A uniform in the Reichsheer. For formal occasions the normal dress jacket was worn, though with a white cloth collar and white gloves. An additional component of the first-class mess uniform was the large medal ribbon.

Right: First Lieutenant Wrede of Infantry Regiment 2 wears the small medal ribbon on his dress jacket. Regimental numbers on the shoulder pieces and the star of rank for officers were made of yellow metal.

shoulder straps on the uniform. Enlisted men wore field gray, non-commissioned officers and officers up to the rank of colonel silver, and generals gold shoulder straps, each with two bars (see picture on page 9). To indicate the service arm and the troop unit, non-commissioned officers and men wore removable oval sleeve badges on their upper sleeves. The white service-arm color was assigned to the infantry as its primary color. Secondary colors made possible a further differentiation of infantry troops such as riflemen (light green/white), pursuit troops (light green/dark green), machine-gun units (light green/golden yellow) etc. Troop units were indicated by Arabic numerals on the sleeve badges.

Above: General of the Infantry Kurt, Baron von Hammerstein-Equord, Chief of the Military Command as of October 1, 1930. The form of the patch and set-in pockets on the dress jacket is easy to see.

Left: General of the Infantry Friedrich W. von Chappuis in his captain's uniform in 1921. On the collar are sewn the silver double braid patches of field gray insignia cloth, on field gray facings.

Left: Parts of imperial uniforms often continued to be worn. Along with the combat jacket, this major wears the old uniform field cap for officers with raised pipings in the service-arm color. New additions were the oak-leaf wreath and the eagle rosette on the piping stripe.

Below: Major General Oppermann, Commander of I.R. 12 from February 1, 1926 to March 31, 1928, wears the prescribed dress cap with gold cap cords and gold pipings of woven braid on the piping stripe and the rim of the peak.

Left: The last form of the Reichswehr dress cap, with embroidered oak-leaf wreath and metal rosette. The later Luftwaffe major and holder of the Knight's Cross, Hugo Paul, wore his own cap in this form in 1933 as a grenadier in I.R. 15.

In the temporary Reichswehr, a new combat jacket was introduced that was to differ from that of the later Reichsheer only in its arched sleeve cuffs. Its clearest identifying marks were the two patch breast pockets, which had been unknown on German uniform jackets until then. Eight buttons and diagonally cut set-in side pockets are further identifying marks of this combat jacket, which was worn particularly by generals until the end of World War II. The basic material and collar of the combat jacket was field gray, and only at the beginning of the Thirties was the collar given a bluish, dark green color. Between the dress and class A jackets and the "single jacket" of the non-commissioned officers and men there was only a difference in the quality of the material, plus more expensive effects. In appearance, all Reichsheer jackets were the same. One exception was

Above: The "undress jacket" M of 1915 for officers and officials of officers' rank could be worn by Reichswehr officers until the beginning of the Thirties. Since December 1923, sewn-on double patches and buttons were used, as on the cloth jacket, instead of service-arm facings on the collar. Lieutenant Werner Gebb of I.R. 118 (4th Grand Ducal Hessian) wore the undress officer's jacket of the imperial army in 1919.

Left: Captain Werner Gebb in 1931. Later major general and commander of various infantry regiments in World War II, Gebb is here wearing the dress cap of field gray knitted fabric, as was prescribed for the Reichsheer since July 1927. Along with the introduction of officers' cords went the change of color on the piping stripe from field gray to bluish dark green.

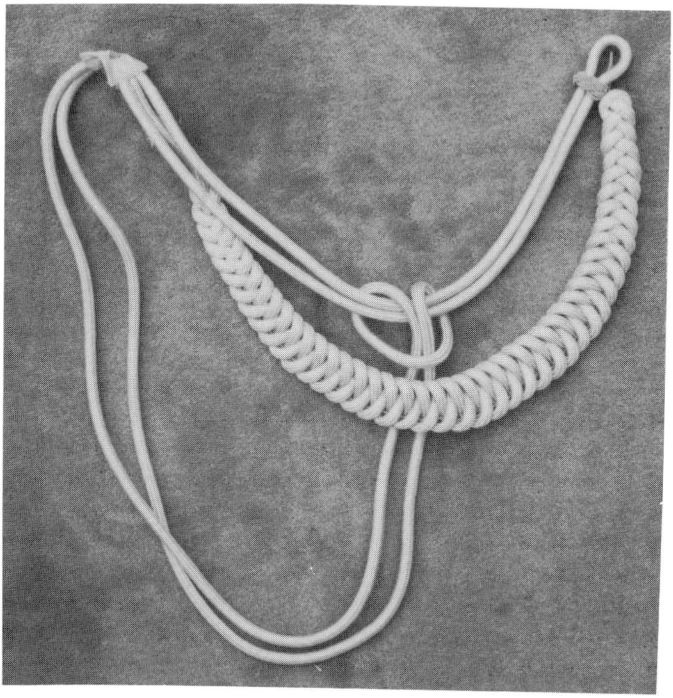

With the creation of the mess jacket for officers in July of 1927, the shoulder band was also introduced. For officers up to the rank of colonel, it consisted of bright silver cord, and for generals, of golden cord. The flat cord plait had a width of 1.5 cm at the ends and 3 cm in the middle, and was made of a 5-mm spun cord. Adjutants wore two additional cords on their shoulders, with bars that hung forward in different lengths.

Lieutenant Gebb's wedding party on October 15, 1927, with several officers wearing the new mess jacket.

the mess jacket for officers, which was introduced in July of 1927; another was the white jacket for officers and officials of officers' rank as of November 1931.

For anyone that would like more thorough information about the uniforms of the German army, which from 1921 to 1935 consisted of only 100,000 volunteers with at least twelve years of service, the following book is recommended: *Schlicht-Kraus, Die Uniformierung und Ausrüstung des deutschen Reichsheeres, 1919-1932,* Ingolstadt 1987.

Above: Captain Werner Gebb in the Reichswehr mess jacket. It differed from the dress jacket in having raised pipings in the service-arm color running down both front edges of the jacket. In addition, the bright silver embroidered patches on the collar were made on facings in the service-arm color. The buttons were bright silver instead of matt white, and bright silver cords were used for the shoulder patches. The mess uniform also included white gloves, a white cloth collar and trousers with pipings in the service-arm color.

Right: A major of pursuit forces (green service-arm color) in a mess uniform with the shoulder band for officers, made of silver braid.

General Heye and his Uniforms

As the third chief of the military command, Lieutenant General Wilhelm Heye succeeded the fallen "Creator of the Reichswehr", Senior General Hans von Seeckt, on October 8, 1926. For about four years, until October 31, 1930, Heye, who was promoted to General of the Infantry as well as the third chief of the military command, was to guide the fate of the Reichsheer. Born on January 31, 1869, he became a lieutenant in 1888 and took part in the fighting in German Southwest Africa in 1906 as a captain. After rising to the highest command positions in World War I, took a position as chief of the operations department in the supreme military command in September of 1918. He became Seeckt's successor as chief of staff in the AOK North.

Further high points of his career: Chief of the troop office from 1920 to 1922 and chief of the army's personnel office. In 1923 the lieutenant general became the commander of Defense Region I, until as General of the Infantry he took over the position of

The chief of the military command loved to ride white horses whenever he carried out his duties on horseback. The advantage was clear, for he could thus be "sighted" from a long way off. The horse had a decisive significance in the Reichsheer, since motorization was only in its beginnings.

the chief of the military command.

Heye retired as a senior general on October 31, 1930. He was retained on the army list as the chief on Infantry Regiment I and thus retained the right to wear the regimental uniform with special general's shoulder patches (see p. 52). During his military career General Heye received many decorations, as the photos show.

General Heye died in 1947 in Braunlage.

Two well-known photos of General Heye, showing him in different general's uniforms. Above: The dress jacket for generals had matt-gold grained buttons as of 1927. Before that, generals wore the matt-white buttons used by officers. Also used since 1927 were the facings for Larisch embroidery in red and the collar of bluish dark green insignia cloth.

Left: The general's jacket had bright red pipings on the right and left front edges since 1927. General Heye wore the jacket without patch breast pockets.

This 1927 photo shows General of the Infantry Heye wearing all of his decorations. He is wearing the general's jacket as a full mess uniform. The aiguilette as well as the gloss gold buttons and the large medal ribbon were prescribed for the full mess uniform. The same applies to the crosses worn around the neck and the stars of the awarded decorations.

Senior General Wilhelm Heye, circa 1937, in the service jacket of the Wehrmacht. He wears the brown leather strap and the small medal ribbon, as well as medals worn around the neck and pinned-on crosses as prescribed along with the peaked cap of the muster uniform. The general also wears the service jacket of the 1st Infantry Regiment (its number is on the shoulder pieces) with a general's rank insignia.

The Steel Helmet from 1916-1945

The headgear of the time was unsuitable for the trench warfare of 1915, and the weaknesses of the leather helmets used by the Germans became obvious very quickly. The shrapnel effect of bursting shells resulted in an increase in severe head injuries, since the Pickelhaube would not deflect even the smallest piece of a shell. Moved by the severity of the head injuries and their effects on the soldiers, Professor Dr. Bier, at that time the naval Surgeon-General and advisory surgeon to the Eighteenth Army Corps, urged the introduction of a protective steel helmet.

In September of 1915 the Uniform Department of the War Ministry began to develop the steel helmet. Under the guidance and cooperation of Artillery Captain Schwerd, in civilian life a professor at the Technical College of Hannover, the M 16 steel helmet took shape. Given the designation of "steel protective helmet", it was first used before Verdun in February of 1916. At the same time, a forehead shield (5) was introduced as auxiliary helmet armor, but it could only be worn for a short time on account of its weight and thus was used only in special action (in trench warfare, by observers, etc.). All steel helmet models used in World War I can be told from later types easily by their noticeable ventilators (1). To make the helmet wearable at all, it had to be fitted with a lining that was attached by means of two side (2) pins and one at the rear. The chinstrap (3) had its own special attachments (4), the so-called 91

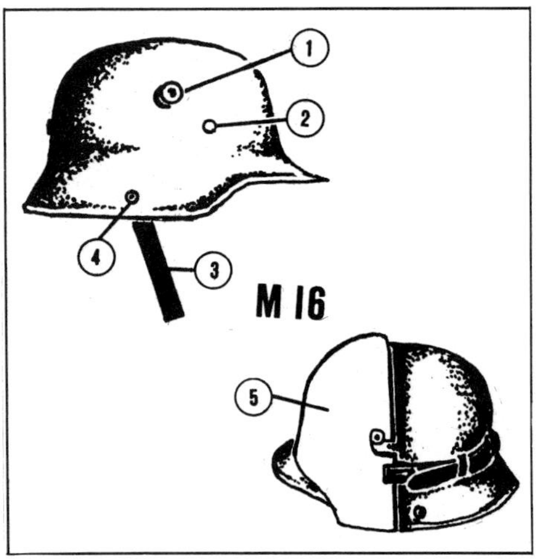

German President Field Marshal von Hindenburg talking with General of the Infantry Heye, who is wearing an M 18 steel helmet.

The Chief of the Military Command, General von Seeckt, inspects newly arrived soldiers. They are wearing M 16 steel helmets. These are Prussian troops, as the emblems on their helmets show. Left: Colonel von Rundstedt, Commander of I. R. 18.

Below: General of the Infantry Heye inspecting an infantry regiment. The second officer from the right wears the open 1928 "experimental jacket."

hooks, which had been introduced on the M 1891 leather helmet. During the war, the lining and the chinstrap were changed. In the M 17 and M 18 steel helmets, the strap was attached directly to the ring of the lining. After the artillery had covered their guns with camouflage paint in 1917, which entered the army's history as "mimicry", various front-line units used this type of painting on their steel helmets. With the partial introduction of the M 18 helmet, which was officially designated a telephone and cavalry helmet as well as a helmet with ear cutouts, the first phase of German steel helmet development came to an end. In all, some 7.5 million helmets and 50,000 forehead shields were manufactured by the end of World War I.

During the Reichswehr era, the M 16 and M 18 models remained in use and were given state emblems on their left sides as of 1923. The coat of

The M 16 steel helmet, recognizable by the projecting ventilators and the chinstrap attachment on the lining.

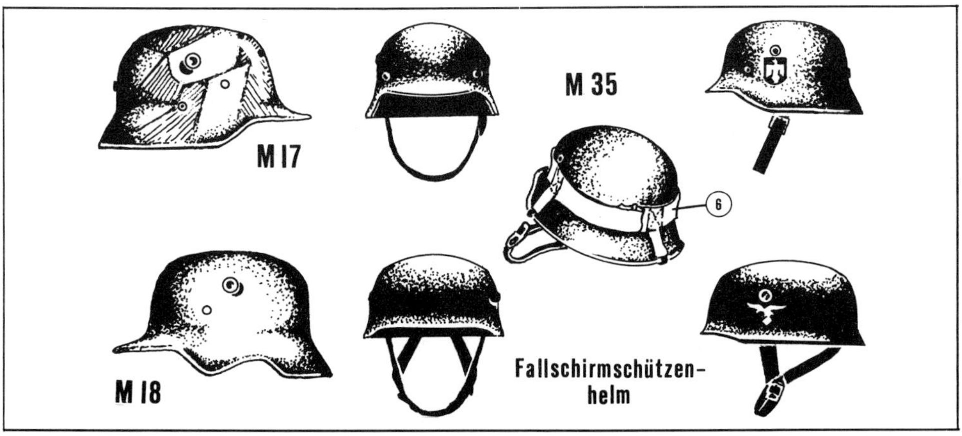

For maneuvers with two parties before World War II, a 4-cm band, woven on both sides, was placed around the helmet; it was red on one side and yellow on the other. The red side wore their color turned to the outside, and those men put out of action turned the band over. The shortened neck protector and a special lining produced the paratrooper's helmet.

arms, about 3.5 cm high and 3.4 cm wide, was simply painted onto the steel helmet. The later emblems (as of 1934), on the other hand, were adhesive labels that were attached 3 millimeters below the ventilator or air opening.

At the beginning of the Thirties, the suggestions for the steel helmet expressed by the troops were first taken into consideration by the Reichswehr command. The chief complaints concerned the heavy weight, the poor hearing (echoes), and the difficulty in seeing when operating, aiming and firing with optical devices.

After several experiments, a new model was introduced in June of 1935. The new M 35 steel helmet had a somewhat higher and shorter brim, new ventilators, and a modernized lining.

Made of 1.1- to 1.2-mm sheet steel in seven steps, without a seam, the M 35 was an improvement that, to be sure, did not offer ideal protection or rule out further limitations. The German steel helmet's greatest handicap was its shape, with its sharply rising silhouette. It almost always offered arriving bullets and shell fragments an acute angle and thus a better possibility of penetration than, for example, a flatly arched helmet shape.

These World War II experiences led in 1944 to the development of a new model, which was to be issued in 1945. At the present time the troops of the East German National People's Army wear this helmet. Before the end of World War II, two other models came into use along with the M 35, one being the "steel helmet for paratroop riflemen", introduced in 1938 with a special lining and issued

The army's silver eagle, used as its helmet badge as of March 1934. On the right side, as of February 17, 1934, there was the national color badge in rounded form. Unlike the eagle emblem worn on the breast, the helmet eagle faced heraldically to the right. Worn on the left side, he was supposed to look forward.

Major Paul Scheuerpflug with the M 35 steel helmet in 1937.

to the men of the paratroop infantry battalion, and later to the pursuit paratroopers.

After the maneuvers of the Thirties had become a serious business, the first difficulties in obtaining materials set in in 1943, and attempts were made to produce the steel helmet with less work. Among these measures were the omission of the rim border and of the national emblem, as well as the reduction in size of the diameter and the stages involved, which resulted in a weight decrease from 2 to 1.7 kilograms per helmet.

Since no provisions originally existed for affixing camouflage material to disguise the round shape of the helmet in the country, the infantrymen made do with various substitutes, such as with a wire cover (7) into which twigs and grass could be stuck. In 1942 this problem was solved with camouflage nets and cloth covers printed in camouflage colors. It must also be noted that all German types of steel helmets were worn by all branches of the Wehrmacht until the end of World War II.

Captain Karl A. Keerl wearing the M 43 steel helmet without a national emblem.

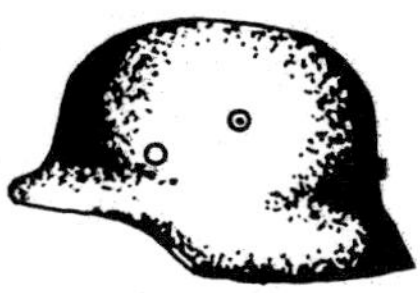

M 43

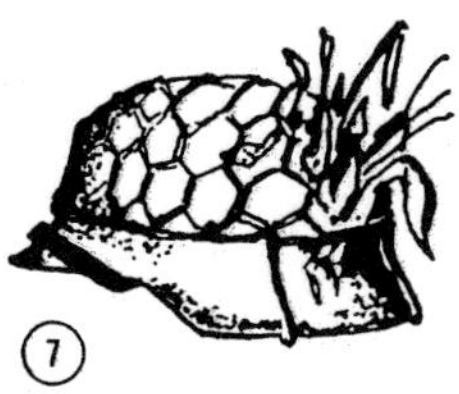

(7)

(8)

The Infantry Flag

Between World War I and 1936 the German Army had no flag. With a decree made a year after the establishment of the "Wehrmacht", the Führer and Supreme Commander of the Wehrmacht created military flags on March 16, 1935. Based on a design by the Berlin commercial artist Paul Casberg, the army flags were then made and turned over to army units by Hitler at the Reich Party Day in Nürnberg on September 14, 1936. Every battalion and every unit of the army was to receive a flag. By May of 1941, great numbers of flags had been provided. Newly created units then no longer received flags, and the final distribution was to be done after the war ended. Even when new service-arm colors were used, which happened often enough when units were newly formed or reorganized, flags

"I swear by God this sacred oath of unqualified obedience to the Leader of the German Reich and people, Adolf Hitler, the Supreme Commander of the Wehrmacht, and will be ready at any time to risk my life for this oath as a brave soldier." There was much discussion of this personified form of the oath after the war. For the infantrymen of I.R. 115 there was no discussion. Before the introduction of the army flag in March of 1936, an officer held a saber on which the recruits placed their left hand during the oath.

Before the oath-taking, the regimental commander inspects the troops. Beginning with the regimental band, the flag follows with the officers and color guard.

were no longer exchanged. The white infantry flag had a size of 125 by 125 centimeters, was made of white silk with a black Iron Cross and the army eagle emblem in a wreath of oak leaves. By order of September 16, 1944, all flags were to be sent to the arsenal in Berlin, which resulted in almost all troop flags ultimately falling into Russian hands. The newsreel scene in which the flags were thrown in the dirt of Red Square during the victory celebration in Moscow is well known. After that they were taken to the Red Army's Central Museum in Moscow. It is not so well known that some flags, especially those of the Austrian units, could be preserved in the Vienna Arsenal.

The flag of the infantry from 1936 to 1945 had a white field with a black silk Iron Cross.

When marching with the flag, it was to be carried over the shoulder. The color guard company marched in ranks behind the flag. Their bayonets are fixed on their carbines.

Music Goes With It

The regimental musicians wore a field-gray uniform like their comrades, but with one difference: they had "swallows' nest" epaulettes on their shoulders as a sign of their special training. They also differed in ranking. Soldiers up to the rank of administrative corporal were called musician-riflemen etc. The same was done in the classes of non-commissioned officers with and without sword-knot. The musician's rank was always preceded by the word "Musician." The music masters formed a special rank class. They belonged to the non-commissioned officers with sword-knot and held the ranks of staff music master, senior music master and music master. Higher ranks in a musician's career were those of military officials (army).

In terms of uniforms, the music masters were almost equal to officers. They wore the uniform with the service-arm color of their troop unit and the special shoulder patches with additional red color between the flat braids. In the Reichswehr days, the shoulder patches of a music master

Emil Hinz of the 5th Company of the Augsburg Infantry Regiment 40 wore his "swallows' nests" correctly on the armhole seams of his uniform jacket.

3. Emblems for Special Training

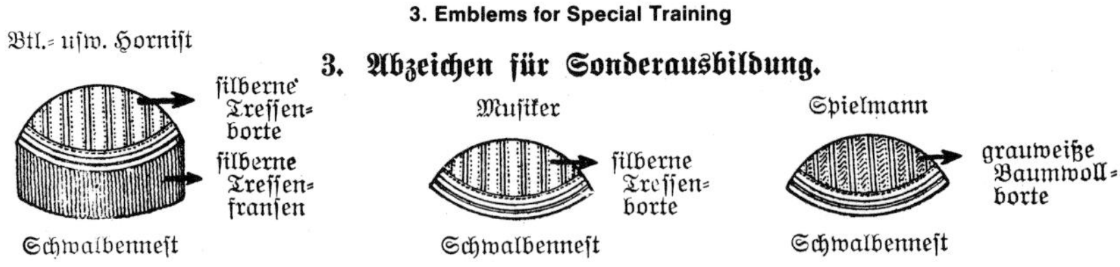

For the infantry, the "swallows' nest" epaulettes of white insignia cloth on a field-gray cloth background with a light lining for stiffening. The seven braid or cotton panels were vertically sewn to the service-arm color background. The border was formed by a crosswise panel or the added fringe of the battalion buglers.

To celebrate the first of May, the 40th Infantry Regiment paraded on the City Hall Square in Augsburg with their complete band. Above the band marches in at the head of the troops. The players, here twelve drummers and twelve fifers, accompany their comrades along with the regimental musicians in the "Prussian step."

consisted of a red braid of three woolen cords side by side. Framed in additional cords, the braid was attached to a service-arm color background. On page 44 the music masters' shoulder patches are shown with the appropriate numbers of the troop units and stars of rank. Within the framework of a further equation to the uniforms and insignia of officers ranks in the mid-Thirties, the lyre was introduced as a career symbol on the shoulder patches and a red flat braid was added to the flat shoulder patches.

As an indication of their special training, the musicians always wore epaulettes on their shoulders. For their cloth jackets and musicians' moleskin jackets, battalion buglers and players had removable epaulettes. They were attached by small hooks on the inside to corresponding eyes on the armhole seams. The epaulettes were made of service-arm color insignia cloth with piping of seven 2.1-cm vertical braid or bars and a closing braid or bar on the lower edge. Players wore light gray bar piping, unlike musicians, for whom silver braid bars of aluminum were used. For the battalion buglers, the epaulettes were also made with 7-cm matt silver fringe. As of 1930 their Class A uniforms, and later their service jackets, had epaulettes sewn onto the armhole seams. In the Twenties, each infantry battalion had a 24-man band with a music master as well as players at the rate of four men per company. With the exceptions of machine-gun and mine-laying companies, each company had two drummers and two buglers. The buglers, simultaneously trained as fifers, carried their signaling bugles

The players of Infantry Regiment 18 have gathered for a photo and set up their instruments, drums and bugles for a "still life."

After a maneuver in Grafenwöhr in 1937, the battalion crescents of the participating battalions were presented. From left to right, the crescents of I.R. 40, 1. Bat./I.R. 91, I.R. 63, and III.Bat./I.R, 91. The troop markings are applied to the crescent standards and engraved on the crescents themselves.

with them even when serving as fifers. The leader of the players was the battalion bugler, who belonged to the battalion staff.

The war brought an end to music at lower troop levels, and in May of 1944 regimental bands were abolished.

From then on, only divisions had small bands.

On maneuvers and in the field, the players and musicians wore no epaulettes. Here the drummers and buglers of an infantry company can be seen.

Insignia of the Third Reich

After the National Socialists came to power in 1933, the eagle rosette of the Weimar Republic was removed from government offices and in the military, and replaced by a black-white-red rosette. One year later the Reich's army and navy were equipped with the national eagle of the Reich. The national emblem of the Reich was the party eagle symbol of the NSDAP with its head turned to the left (heraldic). Since the end of the Twenties, party uniforms had used this eagle on their headgear.

Stylistically changed but still facing left, the eagle was introduced in 1934 to replace the state rosette on headgear and as breast emblems.

The eagles of uniformed government officials, on the other hand, faced right as of 1936, as required.

General of the Infantry Schroth, Commanding General of General Command XII in Wiesbaden, wore his service jacket in 1938 with a national eagle that was very made to be very plastic and three-dimensional. The scalloped form of the patch breast pockets is also unusual.

Gold and poppy red (intense red) were the colors for Reichsheer and Wehrmacht army generals since July 22, 1927. As insignia cloth for shoulder-patch backgrounds, collar panels and jacket piping as well as trouser stripes, poppy red was prescribed. At the same time, buttons and cap cords were gold. When the national eagle was introduced, Generals were given hand-embroidered eagles in gold on dark green cloth backgrounds, using metal thread. Here is the front and back of such an eagle from prewar days. Using rolled sheet gold in plate or foil, a thread was spun around it that combined the advantages of saving material and the utilization of good workmanship. Diagonally or vertically spun threads created the different color effects after embroidery. The back of the eagle was covered with paper to avoid discoloring the uniform.

A hand-embroidered eagle for officers, made of silver-colored metal thread. For officers' national eagles, aluminum foil was generally used for the metal thread. Along with its inexpensive production, aluminum offered the advantage of not oxidizing immediately and becoming unsightly, as silver does. Aluminum thread was used more and more before World War II for many such items whose basic color was silver. Different directions in which the aluminum foil was spun around the thread produced varying optical effects that gave the national eagle, here set off with woolen thread, its vividness. Hand-embroidered means that the work was done by hand with the help of an embroidering machine, with single threads being guided by hand over a cardboard pattern. Under the bluish dark green background of insignia cloth was a gauze lining that held the embroidery and made neat work possible. Below, unlike the hand-embroidered eagles for officers, non-commissioned officers and enlisted men wore machine-embroidered or woven eagles that were made with glossy yarn or matt cotton, or even synthetic thread.

Increasing quantitative needs and material problems with insignia during World War II led to a wide variety of ways to make the national eagle with little expense and labor and with available materials. Hand-embroidery was least well-suited for large quantities, leaving only machine embroidery and weaving to make the national emblem. Here are the front and back of a machine-woven eagle, such as were worn by the millions on combat jackets since the middle of the war. The thread used was synthetic, in this case artificial silk, with matt coloring.

The material shortages during the war also affected the insignia of generals. In comparison to the quantities needed for the rest of the troops, there was no great work-time problem involved here, so hand-embroidery could still be used. Gold was in short supply, and so artificial silk yarn was used. Above is such an example, made of synthetic silk yarn. Going further into synthetic materials led to the use of cellon, a cellulose-based synthetic material, also known as cellglass. Suitably colored and spun around a thread, cellon can be worked well, as the national eagle below shows. The bluish dark green background of the eagle, made of wool, suggests that it was made at the end of the war.

The Officer's Braid

Aiguilettes are known in almost all the world's armies and are still worn to this day. Thus they are not a German invention, though Prussian uniform development during the last century set the style for Europe and to some extent overseas, and the Prussian-German army had introduced aiguilettes for generals and officers by the end of World War I. In the first days of the Weimar Republic, this symbol of the officer was no longer wanted, and only with the creation of a mess uniform in 1927 did the aiguilette return. Unlike that of the imperial army, the gold aiguilette for generals and the silver one for officers were made of only one braid, which was worn around the right shoulder.

With the introduction of the 1935 service jacket, which embodied a return to the old Prussian uniform tradition, the "Shoulder band of the system time", as it was called in National Socialist Party terminology, was changed to the old Prussian form. Two braids of gold metal cord for generals and silver aluminum cord for officers now decorated the right side of the jacket. They went with the parade uniform and the first- and second-class mess uniforms. They

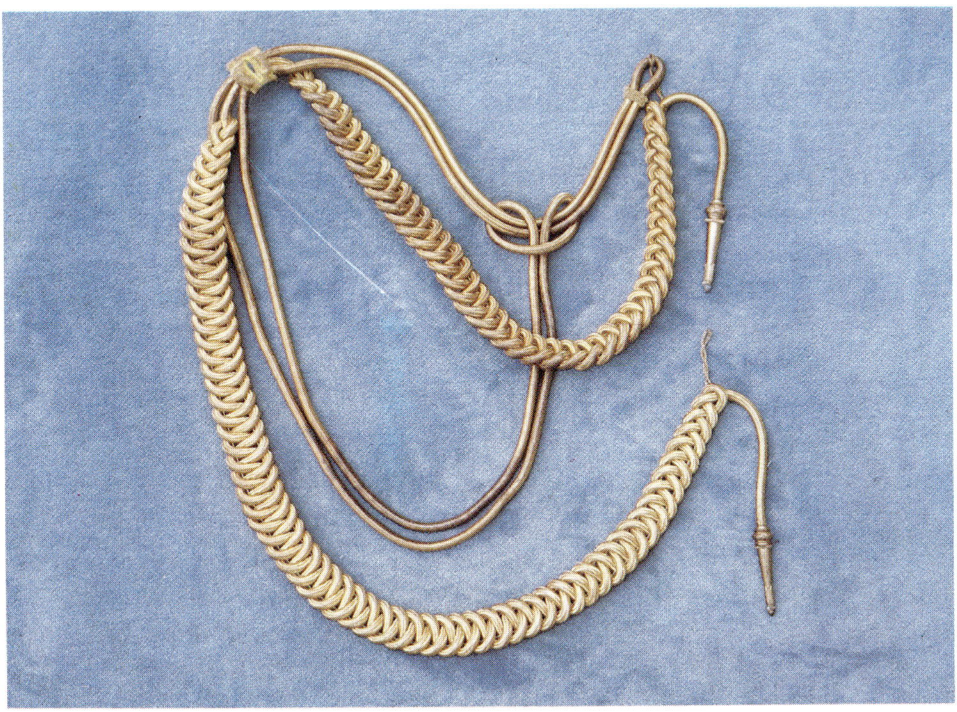

The aiguilette for generals of the army, used from the mid-Thirties to 1945.

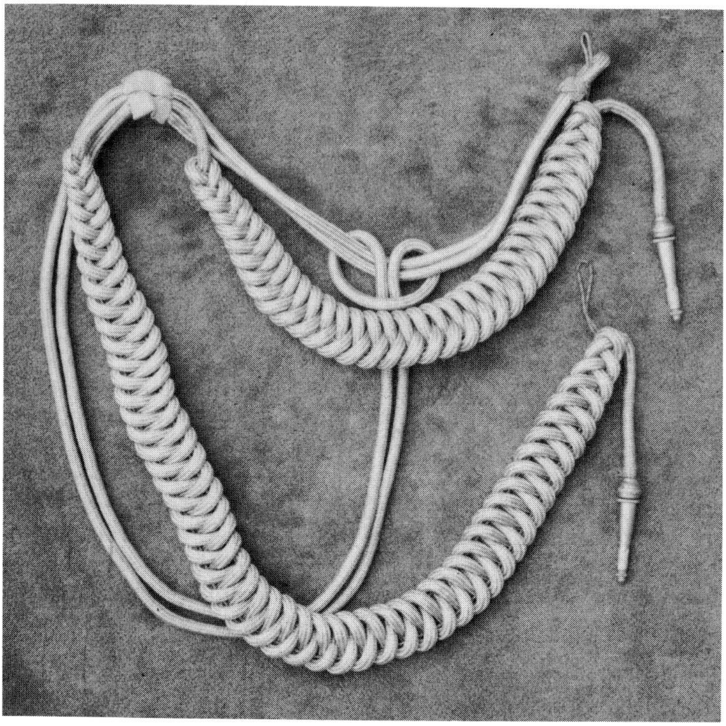

With the introduction of the mess jacket for the Reichsheer in July of 1927, generals and officers were issued aiguilettes (see also page 14). When the Wehrmacht army was allowed to wear the dress jacket as part of parade, Class A and mess uniforms, the aiguilette was changed. Instead of one, now two wide cords of spun metal were worn on the right breast. The silver aiguilette for officers up to and including the rank of colonel consisted of silver-colored aluminum cords.

were never worn, though, on overcoats. The way the aiguilette was worn on the dress jacket is easy to see in the photo on page 39. A 4-mm cord had an aluminum weave spun around it, giving the whole a diameter of 5.5 mm. This cord was then braided and worked into the aiguilette. The two ends of the cord ended in aluminum-colored end caps. The aiguilettes made for generals, originally gold-plated, were replaced even before the war, for reasons of cost, by cellon material, which had the advantage of not oxidizing. In 1938 the music masters received red braided aiguilettes.

Originally, only the officers' brown leather belt could be worn with the dress jacket for parades. By order of July 1937, the field belt was introduced, with a gold buckle for generals and a silver buckle for officers. The material of the field belt was made of aluminum thread and had dark green stripes.

This photo of a wedding party before World War II shows the bridegroom in a first-class mess uniform with dress jacket and aiguilette, plus the army service medal for four years' service as a large medal ribbon. At right next to him is a Luftwaffe officer in a first-class evening uniform with white bow tie and vest plus aiguilette, which was made of only one braided cord for the Luftwaffe. He also wears long cloth trousers with piping plus a large medal ribbon.

Side Arms and Company Sword Knots

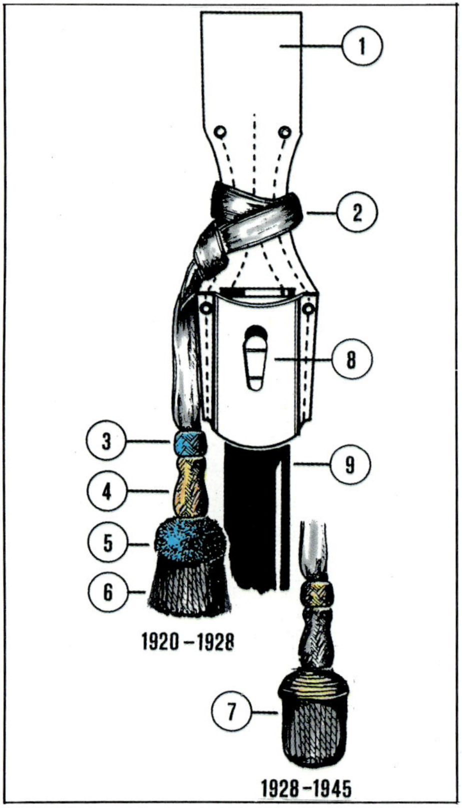

Until 1945, all ranks of the infantry were equipped with bare side arms (bladed weapons). Non-commissioned officers and men carried bayonets and officers wore sabers. In 1935 officers also were issued army officers' daggers, and non-commissioned officers with sword knots were allowed to wear a saber. Until World War I a certain usefulness of these bladed weapons could not be denied, but after that they degenerated into mere uniform decorations, and daggers and sabers were no longer used in the Bundeswehr, unlike the National People's Army of the DDR.

A particular form of side weapon is the bayonet, which when fitted onto the rifle became a stabbing weapon in close combat. Since all non-commissioned officers and men were equipped with them, the sword-knot was suited to be used as an identifying mark of one's company affiliation.

The sword-knot for enlisted infantrymen had a white woolen braid band (2) that, in the form shown here, was slung around the side-arms scabbard (1). The slide (3) and the crown (5) showed the color of the company. The staff (4) was made in the color of the company. The color of the brush (6) matched that of the braid band. As of 1928 the open brush was worn until 1945 in closed acorn form (7). A carrying hook (8) is shown on the mouth shield of the scabbard (9).

A chart of the color symbols for the companies of an infantry regiment.

Parts of the Army Officer's Dagger of 1935

1. Plastic handle
2. Handle ring
3. Crossguard
4. Bumper
5. Blade with trade mark
6. Handle knob
7. Mouth plate with spring and screws
8. Metal sheath
9. Bands
10. Carrying rings

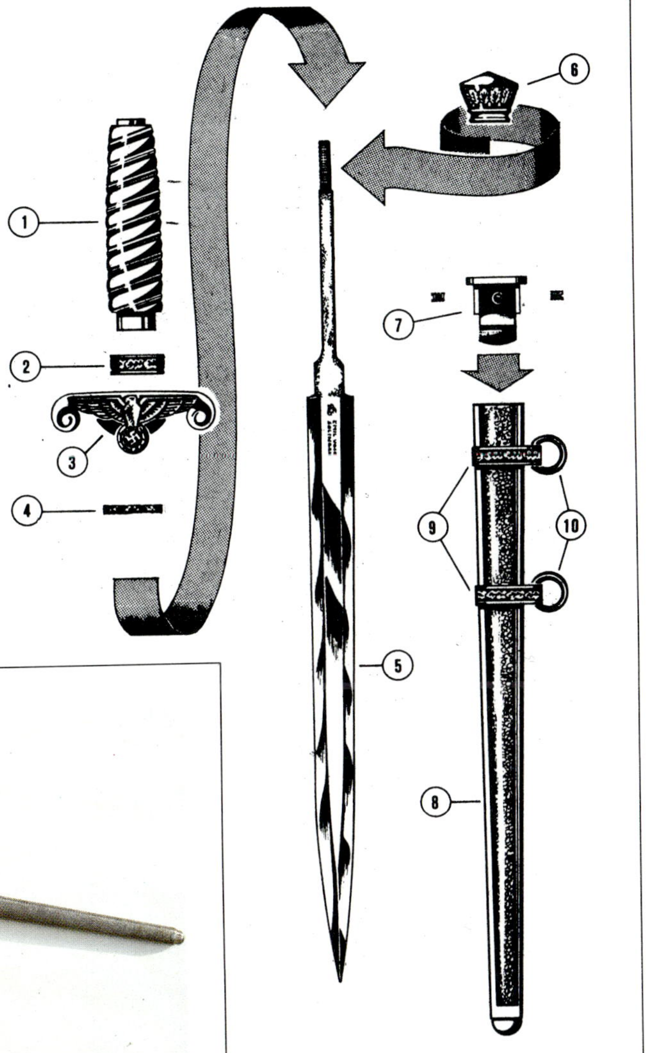

Short steel weapons for officers were unknown in the German army until 1935. Since World War I, all officers wore the officer's saber as a side arm, which was prescribed for certain uniforms. The dagger was added as an auxiliary weapon. The dagger could be worn with the Class A and mess uniforms, the saber only with the parade uniform. The decision in favor of the dagger had not only the needed equipment of prewar days in mind, but also an economic basis. The manufacturers of side arms got bigger orders.

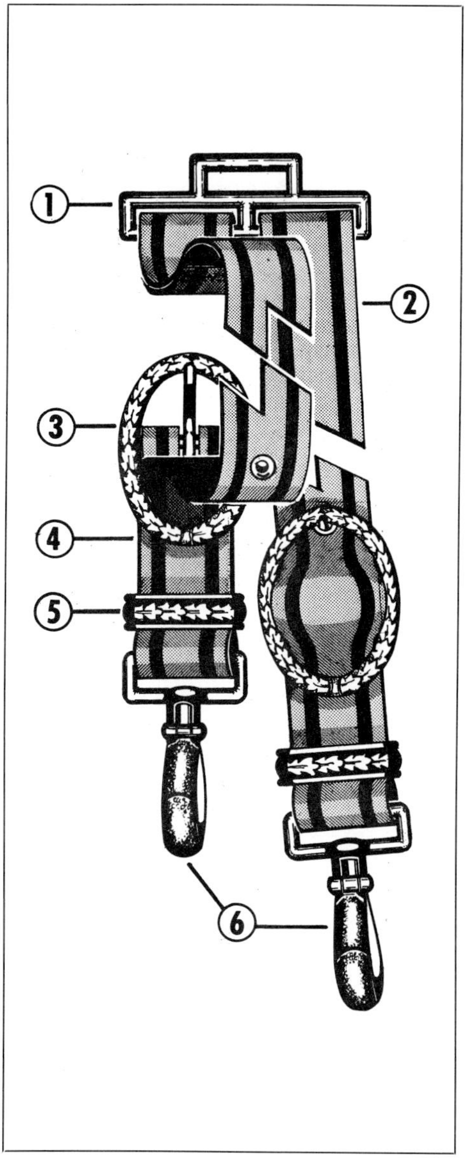

Parts of a dagger strap, by which the dagger could be hooked onto the uniform: 1. Triple eyes, 2. Long hanging strap (dagger holder), 3. Oval clasp, 4. Short hanging strap, 5. Slide, 6. Carbine hooks.

Non-commissioned officers with sword-knots wore their saber scabbards in this manner on their side-arms sheath. The rank class of the non-commissioned officer with sword-knot could wear the non-commissioned officer's saber or side arms on appropriate occasions.

The sword-knot had a colored staff and colored slide and crown. By the color combination, the informed observer could tell which company the wearer belonged to. What with the regimental number on the shoulder patches and the sword-knot, a simple soldier was an "open book." Non-commissioned officers could not be recognized as belonging to any unit by their sword-knot, since the dark green, silver-shot band of braid with its silver fringe or acorn of aluminum cord was the same for all non-commissioned officers. The color code, white for the first unit, red for the second, yellow for the third and blue for the fourth, was introduced in 1808 as part of Prussian army reform. This type of sword-knot was not worn with a saber, which had its own type of attachment. At first the sword-knot, wrapped around the hand, was

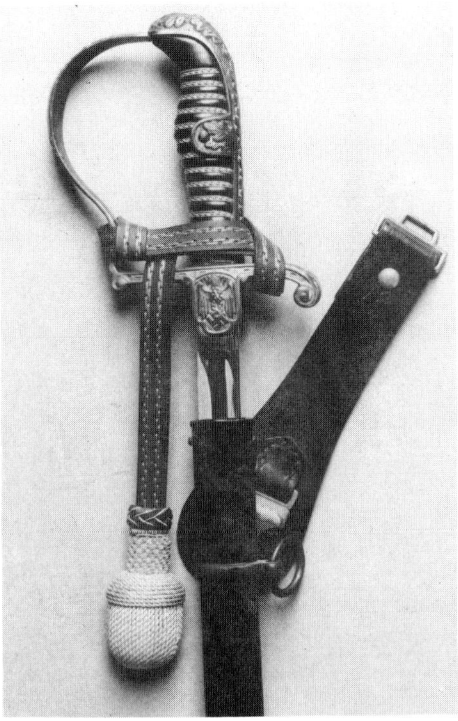

Above: the carrying apparatus and system for holding the saber's scabbard can be seen clearly here. Left: the saber sword-knot in detail.

The way of wearing a saber on an overcoat. The carrier led through the left coat pocket, and the saber was hooked onto it.

supposed to make sure that the weapon did not get lost in battle. The sword-knots for the officer's dagger and the saber were attached to the weapon and thus fulfilled their function in a purely optical way. On side arms, attached to the carbine as an extension of the infantryman's arm, the sword-knot had no actual function, and so it became purely an identifying mark on the side-arms scabbard.

Generaloberst
General der Jnf. usw.
General-leutnant
General-major
Oberst Rw.-Min.
Oberstleutnant Jnfanterie
Major Fahrtruppe
Rittmeister Kavallerie
Hauptmann Zeugamt
Oberleutnant Pioniere
Leutnant Nachr. Truppe
General-stabsarzt
Oberstabsarzt
Stabsarzt
General-veterinär
Oberst-veterinär
Ober-veterinär
Ober-musikmeister Musikdirektor
Ober-musikmeister
Musik-meister
Rw.-Min.
Jnfanterie Oberfeldwebel
Jäger
Kavallerie-Wachtmeister
Artillerie-Unter-wachtmeister
Pioniere Unteroffizier
Nachr.-Truppe Uffz.-Anwärter u. Unterführer
Kraftfahrtruppe
Fahrtruppe
Sanitäts-abteilung
Gruppen-kommando
Wehrkreis-kommando
Kavallerie-Divisionsstab
Jnfanterie-führer
Artillerie-führer
Jnfanterie-schule
Kavallerie-schule
Artillerie-schule
Pionier-schule
Jntendant
Ober-intendantur-inspektor
Stabs-zahlmeister
Oberstabs-apotheker
Heeresmusik-inspizient
Ministerial-direktor
Ministerialrat
Kriegsgerichts-rat
Heeres-unterkunfts-amtsvorsteher
Verwaltungs-inspektor
Back-meister
der Heeresverpfleg.-Ämter
Verwaltungssekr. der Heeresbeklei-dungsämter
Oberverwal-tungssekretär, Lazarett
Waffen-meister
Regiments-sattler

Two charts of the various insignia of rank for the army, from contemporary sources. At left are the shoulder patches and flaps used circa 1930; above, those used circa 1938. The field-gray shoulder flaps of the Reichsheer were dark green in the Wehrmacht army. The difference between shoulder patches of insignia or basic cloth, finished with piping, and shoulder patches of flat metal cord, laid or woven on service-arm color background, is particularly differentiated above. The top two rows show generals' and officers' shoulder patches.

Shoulder Patches and Flaps

After the impracticality of sleeve insignia and stripes as indications of rank in the "clothing of the peacetime army" and the "temporary Reichswehr" had been realized, shoulder patches and shoulder flaps, which had been used in the imperial army, came back into use. After 1921, to be sure, a better terminology was striven for, and so the word "Achsel" was replaced by "Schulter" in the German nomenclature, and this term is still in use. Enlisted men wore their shoulder flaps, bordered in their service-arm color, with attached regimental number, plus the corporal's chevron of braid on their left upper arm as their insignia of rank. The sixty-degree

Above: On the combat jacket with square-cut shoulder flaps, the non-commissioned officer's braid ran along the lower collar edge, unlike the service jacket, where they were sewn on, as prescribed, to the upper collar edge.

Left: Adam Dyroff, later major and commander of the Third Battalion of Armored Grenadier Regiment 115, received the Knight's Cross of the Iron Cross in December in recognition of his bravery. Here he is shown as a rifleman of I.R. 115.

Right: Shoulder flap for a student of the non-commissioned officer school (US) at Eutin (E), which existed along with 21 other schools in June of 1944 to train junior leaders.

angle of braid, with its point downward, was sewn onto a field-gray and later dark green background and then onto the uniform jacket. From non-commissioned officers upward, the shoulder flaps and patches were the only places for emblems of rank and troop. Service-arm color pipings and backgrounds for shoulder patches were introduced in the Reichsheer and are still customary today, as the Bundeswehr shoulder patches show, though there have been a few interruptions and exceptions. Until May of 1945, the non-commissioned officer without sword-knot could be recognized by the open braid on the armhole seams. For a staff sergeant, the braid ran all around the shoulder flap, and for the non-commissioned officer with sword-knot, the rank from technical sergeant up was indicated by white metal stars on and between the braid. Officers wore shoulder patches of smooth or braided metal cords with gold metal stars of rank and regimental numbers as well as other symbolic letters. Since the

During the French campaign, Baron Gerd von Ketelhodt was recognized for exceptional bravery. As First Lieutenant and Chief of the 9th Company of I.R. 472, he was awarded the Knight's Cross on July 13, 1940. For reasons of camouflage, the regimental numbers were removed or covered in combat. Upper right: Shoulder patch of a captain in I.R. 5.

Below: Lower-level sergeants, including officer candidates, in a recruiting office in Army Zone 4, wore these flaps. Non-commissioned officers wore their insignia on their shoulder flaps with white metal braid edging. Under the stylized W is the Roman numeral indicating the zone.

Above: The soldiers of the recruiting offices did not necessarily belong to the infantry. But at the beginning of the war they were given the white service-arm color. This is the shoulder flap of an enlisted man's rank with sewn-on symbols.

Above: Left shoulder patch of a major in the recruiting office of Zone 10. The shiny aluminum braid and the gold-colored symbols with polished edges suggest that it was a shoulder patch for a service jacket or combat jacket with piping.

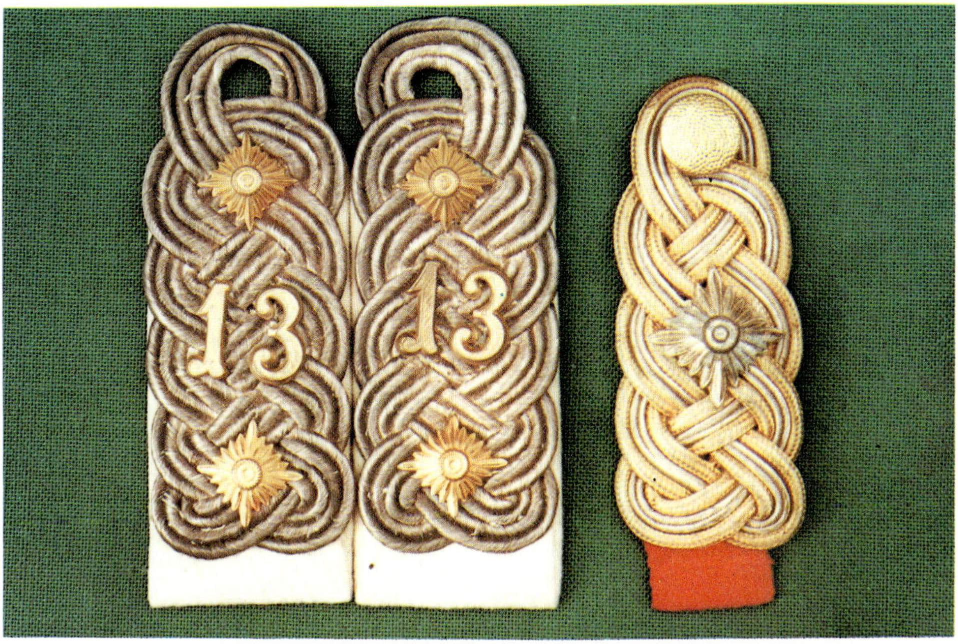

Reichswehr shoulder patches (round-cut numbers) of Colonel Hahn (died 1936), Commander of I.R. 13, and the same officer's later shoulder patch as a lieutenant general.

introduction of the mess jacket in the Reichsheer, and especially since the restoration of the service jacket, shiny aluminum shoulder patches with polished stars and symbols have been sewn to the armhole seams. For the combat uniform, the flat cords of the shoulder patches remained in matt colors. Buttoned-on patches were common on coats, though sewing was the most commonly used means of attachment and was required for some uniforms.

Matt silver shoulder patches for the combat jacket of a major, with the new (straight) numerals used shortly before World War II.

Insignia for Special Service Positions

The Larisch embroidery on generals' combat and service jacket collar panels can be regarded as an indication of a special service position.

Medical and veterinary officers as well as military officials at general's rank likewise wore this embroidery. Staff officers as well as chief officials in the Reich War Ministry had matt gold embroidery on their collar panels. Officers of the general staff had silver-colored embroidery instead. In addition, the generals wore 2-mm poppy-red pipings on their trousers, as well as 40-mm piping stripes (called Lampassen) in the same color on either side of the piping itself. For general staff members and officers of the Reich War Ministry, the pipings and stripes consisted of carmine-colored insignia cloth. The adjutant's emblem for officers, a flat-braided loop of round 6-mm aluminum cord, was introduced in the Reichsheer in July of 1927.

Non-commissioned officers also had a special emblem for their position. Since July of 1922 the master sergeants serving with the troops, better known as "company mothers", wore two non-commissioned officers' braids around their sleeve cuffs of their jackets. Five millimeters from the upper edge of the cuff and the same distance from each other, these stripes were also called "piston rings." Soldiers who were appointed to serve as non-commissioned officers' orderlies wore a non-commissioned officer's braid on the edge of their collars, in front of the collar panel and on the lower edge of it until its end, from their appointment until their promotion to non-commissioned officers. At the same time they wore a loop of braid on the lower end of the shoulder flap. Those of the junior leader class wore only this braid loop.

For the special training of non-commissioned officers and men, which was concluded with an examination, there were round emblems with a diameter of about 55 mm that were used since December of 1920 and were made originally of field-gray

Senior corporal and non-commissioned officer's orderly (with a loop on the shoulder flap) with the emblem for signal and intelligence personnel, at the flasher lamp, circa 1936. On his lower arm this senior corporal wears the bar for first-class shooting, which was introduced in 1928.

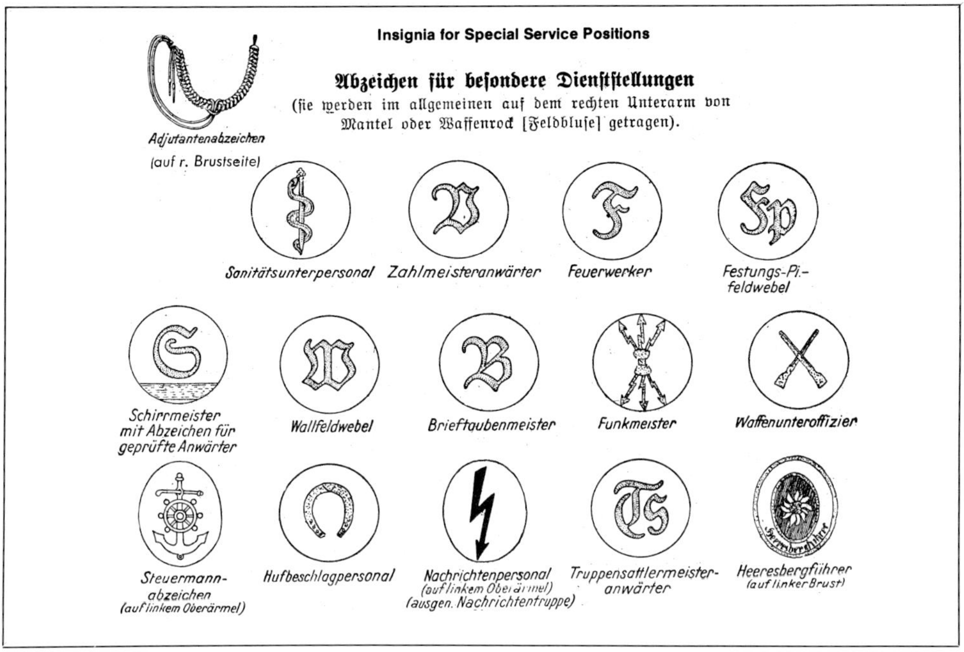

This illustration from the 1937-38 "Reibert" (Service Instruction in the Army) shows the insignia for special service positions.

and later of dark green insignia cloth. The round discs included yellow embroidered Gothic letters and symbols for the wearer's special training. They were worn on the lower right arm of the jacket and coat ten millimeters above the cuff.

With the exception of the intelligence troops, the signal and intelligence personnel of all other troops wore, as of 1924, a lightning bolt in the service-arm color on an oval background as an emblem of their special training. This was worn on the upper left arm. As of 1939, if the wearer of this emblem held an appointment, then the emblem was edged in silver.

Proper position of the adjutant's braid on the right shoulder and breast side.

Regimental Uniforms for Generals

Until the end of World War I it was customary in the German army to grant the honor of being regimental chief to highly-placed persons. Without any requirement to administer or command, ruling princes, members of princely houses and generals were honored by being named to the small group of regimental chiefs, whose regiments often bore their names. After 1918 no more regimental chiefs were named, and only a few retired generals were given the right to wear the uniform of a regiment to which they were closely linked.

Generals who were granted the right to wear a regimental uniform were carried on the regimental roster until their death. In 1938 there were 28 retired generals and four in active service who were so honored. Along with the right to wear the uniform, the leaders of the Third Reich also named distinguished generals to be regimental chiefs. Of the six regimental chiefs, four belonged to the infantry and one each to the artillery and cavalry.

Named as regimental chiefs for the infantry were: Senior General von Seeckt (I.R. 67), Field Marshal von Rundstedt (I.R. 18), General of the Infantry Ritter von Epp (I.R. 61) and

General of the Infantry Erich Wöllwarth commanded the 4th Division in the Reichsheer and was commander of War Zone IV. Retired on January 1, 1929 as General of the Infantry, he became honorary General of the Infantry on September 1, 1940. Previously he had been granted the right to wear the regimental uniform of I.R. 15. Left: The general's shoulder patch with white background, from his service jacket.

Generals with the right to wear the regimental uniform were only recognizable from the other regimental officers by their shoulder patches. They wore the regimental numbers on the general's patches. Here is the service jacket of General of the Infantry Erich Wöllwarth.

Field Marshal von Rundstedt wears the general's cap (field cap) with gold-colored pipings with the uniform of the chief of I.R. 18.

Field Marshal von Blomberg (I.R. 73). Instead of wearing the poppy-red service color of a general, they wore the white of the infantry (piping on the front edge of the jacket, shoulder patches, collar panels).

A very noticeable emblem was the regimental number of gold-colored metal on the general's shoulder patches.

The service jacket corresponded in service color and other details to those of infantry officers. Only the general's shoulder patches on a white background, with the regimental number, indicated the honorary right.

Details of Field Marshal von Rundstedt shoulder patches with attached regimental numerals. The silver-colored marshal's staffs are hollow, as can be seen clearly here, and the added numerals have a golden color.

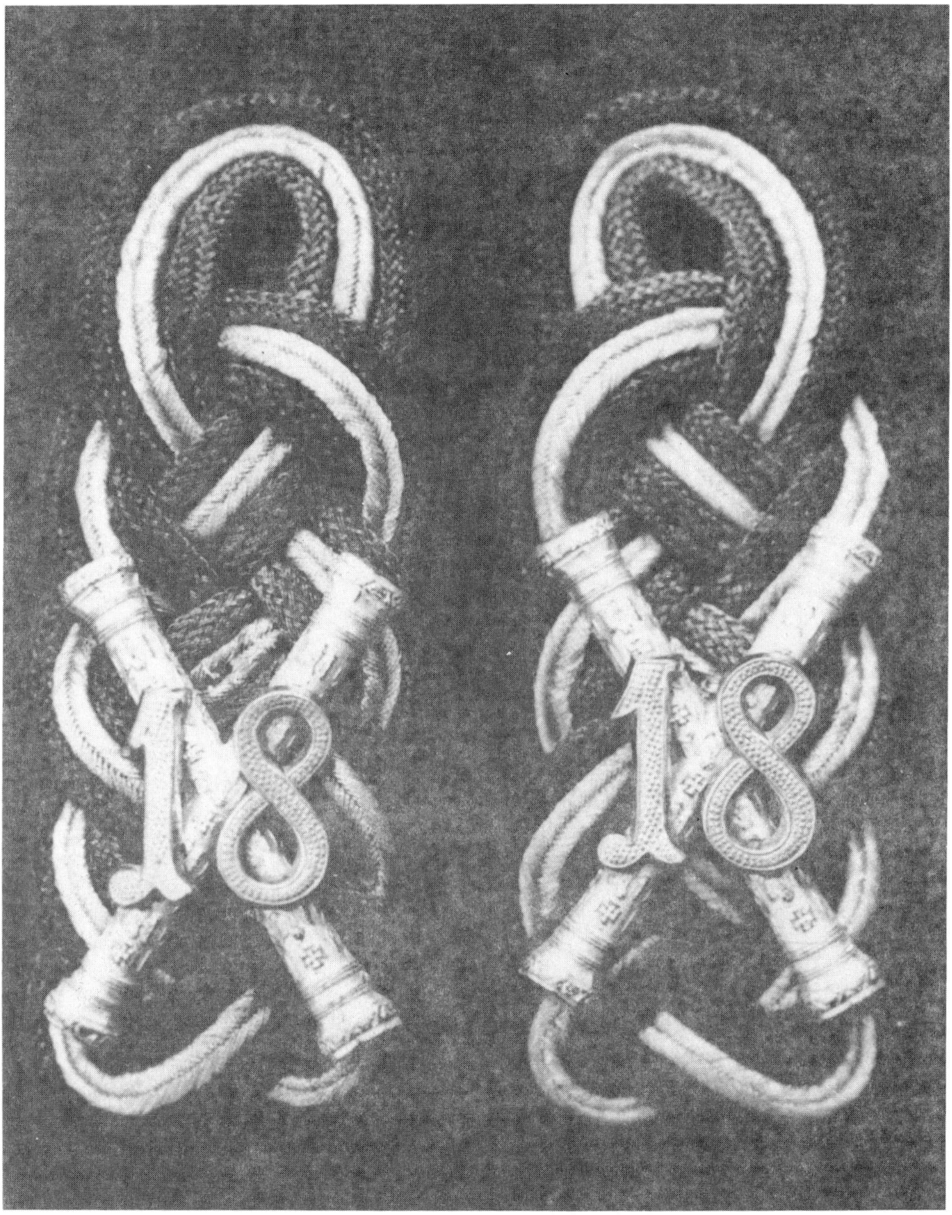

In addition to the way the regimental numbers are attached over the marshal's staffs on the shoulder patches (see upper left photo), Field Marshal von Rundstedt also wore his shoulder patches in this form as regimental chief. He particularly preferred this type for his service jacket.

The national eagle for generals and the collar panels in white service color, as well as the shoulder patches for the standard general's uniform, come from uniforms of Field Marshal von Rundstedt as regimental chief.

Service jacket for generals, this one for a field marshal. The special embroidery on the sleeve panels is noteworthy.

Uniforms in Peace and War

By order of April 1, 1933, the Reichsheer was given a new combat jacket, which was worn in its basic form until the end of World War II. The row of five field-gray buttons on the front, and the four patch pockets, characterized it. In the beginning, the turned-down collar had the field-gray color of the jacket. After September 9, 1935 the collar was made of bluish dark green cloth. To it were sewn the matt silver double bars with service-arm colored stripes on a dark green background. The difference between non-commissioned officers' and enlisted men's combat jackets consisted, in addition to the difference in the quality of the cloth used, in the possibility of attacking side hooks to the enlisted men's jackets to hold the belt better. In the insignia too, there were corresponding differences. The national eagle was hand-embroidered for officers and woven or machine-embroidered for the lower ranks.

Part of a group photo showing details of the service jacket. The trousers go with the combat jacket, since they have no service-color piping. There are also two soldiers, at left center and in the top row, wearing the combat jacket. The way the rifleman's cords, the epaulettes, the corporal's chevron and the private first class's star (first row, far right) were worn, as well as the braid applied to the collars of non-commissioned officers with sword-knot (center), are easy to see.

The introduction of the service jacket on June 29, 1935 was a throwback to old traditions. The soldiers of the Wehrmacht army received a parade and Class A uniform cut in the old Prussian style, without front pockets and with eight shiny silver-colored metal buttons plus embroidered patches on the collar and sleeve panels. The back pockets were each closed by three additional buttons.

The "decorated combat jacket" for officers was introduced in July of 1937 and differed from the regular infantry combat jacket in having white

Army men married in the first-class mess uniform of service jacket with field belt, white gloves and collar tie as well as a large medal ribbon. This photo was taken in 1943 or 1944 and shows the captain's shoulder patches for the infantry (without regimental number) and the following medals: Iron Cross first class (pinned on), Iron Cross second class next to the four-year service medal and the infantry assault badge in silver and the wound medal in black.

Left: Shoulder patch for a captain's service jacket (sewn on), of shiny aluminum flat cord with polished stars and regimental numbers.

Service jacket, here as a first-class mess jacket (officer's shoulder braid), of the infantry captain and later Major General Ivo-Thilo von Trotha of Infantry Regiment 15 (Kassel).

The decorated service jacket, or service jacket with service-color pipings, as a second-class dress uniform of the war-zone commander in Worms, Colonel Karkowski. Worn with shoulder belt before World War II.

Above: For non-commissioned officers and men, cap emblems of metal were prescribed. Another identifying mark of the service cap is a strap of lacquered leather. Sergeant Hugo Paul (holder of the knight's Cross) is shown here in his standard Reicheer jacket with service-color piping.

An infantry colonel in the combat jacket at parade uniform (field tie, large medal ribbon). Instead of a steel helmet, he wears the service cap with metal insignia. The service-color pipings on the piping stripes and in the top seam are easy to see.

Right: Officers' peaked caps with hand-embroidered insignia as used for the service cap before and during the war. Hand-embroidered insignia were only allowed for officers, as well as non-commissioned officers on private caps.

pipings on the edge of the collar, buttonholes and cuffs. The insignia were the same as those on the service jacket.

When World War II broke out, war experiences necessitated a succession of great and small changes, which finally resulted in a new combat uniform. In the Polish campaign of 1939 a particular problem with the regimental numbers on the shoulder patches already appeared. These numbers told enemy spies what troop units were where at the front. Officers began to cover their regimental numbers with an appropriately wide loop of cloth, until the numbers were removed as of 1940. Letters indicating particular troop membership still had their place on shoulder flaps and patches. Midway through the war the

The collar panels of officers with white facings and hand-embroidered double bars of shiny metal thread (aluminum) can be seen clearly here. On the collar of the service jacket and the jacket with pipings, this type of patch was used. The later Lieutenant General Paul Scheuerpflug wears the M 16 steel helmet in this photo. In 1933 Paul Scheuerpflug was a captain on the staff of the First Battalion of I.R. 15. In World War II he served as adjutant of the 35th I.D. and Army Group F. He was also the commander of I.R. 116 and the 68th Infantry Division and was decorated with the oak leaf cluster for the Knight's Cross.

Zur frommen Er=innerung im Gebete an den ehren=ge=achteten Herrn

Daniel Ampenberger

Unteroffizier
bei einem Infanterie=Regiment

Geb. am 1. August 1914 in Freienried
Gefallen im Gefechte bei Brutek südöstl.
von Zamosc am 21. Sept. 1939

O Herr, gib ihm die ewige Ruhe und das ewige Licht leuchte ihm, Herr laß ihn ruhen in Frieden. Amen.

Buchdruckerei Karl Lindner, Friedberg

Left: Death notice of a non-commissioned officer, allowed only at the beginning of the war. The enlisted men's collar panels were almost as wide as those of officers.

On August 22, 1942 the military supreme command gave an order by which the insignia of rank on uniforms or shoulder patches of the German Wehrmacht were regulated. It was also stated: For identification of the ranks of officers and non-commissioned officers on: Winter uniforms.
Snow uniforms, show shirts, anoraks, bare pelts, protective fatigue uniforms for armored troops, rush-green protective uniforms for ordnance maintenance of batteries (E) and 2-cm anti-aircraft guns, protective fatigue uniforms for the crews of armored reconnaissance cars, aviators; protective uniforms for balloon service, tropic shirts, fatigue jackets, training uniforms and jackets for work uniforms are to have special insignia of rank woven on rectangular black backgrounds, golden yellow for generals and light green for the other ranks. The insignia were to be attached to pieces of clothing on the upper left sleeve, with their upper edge ten centimeters from the armhole seam. Here the front and back of the insignia of rank of Major General Werner Gebb are shown. This emblem is not woven, but machine-embroidered with a sewn-on golden yellow braid.

Insignia of rank on pieces of clothing without shoulder patches

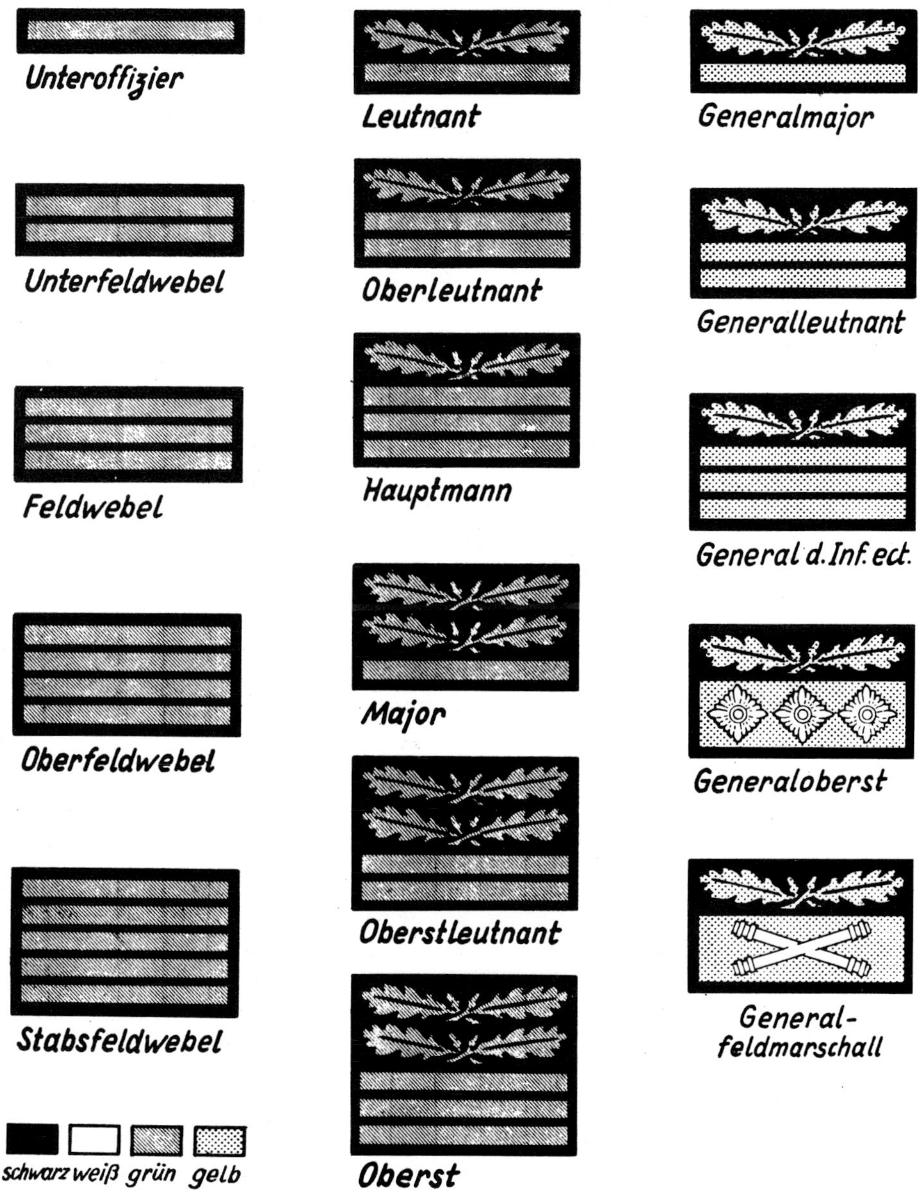

Slip-on loops for shoulder patches. The symbols of Machine-gun Battalion 13 are applied with white synthetic wool thread.

use of sliding loops with unit indication in the service-arm color for non-commissioned officers and men began. Assignments to other troop units could thus be handled quickly and economically.

Next to the steel helmet, the combat cap was the most important headgear at the front. With the combat cap "in boat shape" for all ranks, equipped with a white Soutache angle, the soldiers went into World War II. Officers and generals could choose between two models. A search for a really practical combat cap that was suited to the differing climatic conditions in the various theaters of war in World War II led to the adoption of the undeniably practical "Baschlik

Shoulder patch for a staff sergeant in Infantry Regiment 3. The rank of staff sergeant (3 stars) was introduced in September of 1938.

Left: Slip-on loop for the shoulder flap of a master sergeant of Home Guard Battalion 881 with white symbols. After the abolition of regimental numbers at the beginning of the war, these loops provided necessary identification as of the middle of World War II.

The field cap for officers (new type) was introduced in December of 1938 and had silver pipings of aluminum thread on the top seam and the front flap edge, plus a woven national eagle and a service-color Soutache chevron.

In March of 1934 the officers received a field cap very similar to the peaked cap. It was soft, though, and had woven insignia of aluminum thread. General of the Infantry Karl Hollidt, as commander of the 6th Army in mid-1943, wore this field cap for officers (older type).

Below: The field cap for non-commissioned officers and men of 1934 can be regarded as a forerunner of the new-type field cap for officers.

cap." In the Austrian army this cap was already worn as a combat cap before World War I. Taken over by the mountain troops of the Reichsheer, it enjoyed great popularity during action in the high mountains and in cold stormy weather. Warmly lined inside, it had a longitudinal top the same size as the head width. The flaps (Baschlik) were attached to the lower rim, which rose up to meet the top rim. In front, one or two buttons held the flap ends together. When they were undone, the buttons could be buttoned under the chin, and the flaps and peak provided excellent protection from sun, wind and rain. As the "uniform combat cap", the Baschlik cap entered

During World War II the officers' combat jacket was worn with a brown leather belt with a matt silver two-tongue buckle. Until October of 1939 a brown leather shoulder strap over the right shoulder was part of the combat uniform.

Above: Three types of field cap in one picture. The two grenadiers at left wear the M 1942 field cap with two buttons on the front. In cold weather they held the flaps under the chin. Captain Günther Vollmer, holder of the Knight's Cross and battalion leader of Grenadier Regiment 411, wears the old-type field cap for officers, and at right is the M 1934 field cap.

Right: Along with the uniform field cap 43, this officer's orderly wears the 1943 combat jacket without pocket folds and with field-gray collar.

Below: Woven national eagle with rosette, used on field caps as of 1942.

General of the Infantry von Scheele (left) talking with Major General Werner Gebb in the summer of 1944. General Scheele's breeches with general's stripes are easy to see.

German uniform history in 1943. Worn by all ranks with appropriate insignia and fittings, it was one of the most frequently used types of headgear on the German side in World War II. Material problems and war experiences led in 1942 to the introduction of a new combat jacket. For non-commissioned officers and men, this combat jacket had no pocket folds any more. In addition, the bluish dark green collar was eliminated for all ranks. The collar was made of the same field-gray cloth as the jacket itself.

The double patches were made from then on of field-gray wool with light gray outer and inner panels, with a stripe in the service-arm color only for officers. They were also permitted to continue wearing their old collar panels. The cut of the new combat jacket allowed the jacket to be worn open with shirt and tie. In the last years of the war, this was the usual way for officers to wear the combat jacket.

Under the command of a sergeant, a group of the Third Company of Medical Replacement Section 13 (Bad Kissingen) marches past the photographer in November of 1941. Instead of wearing combat boots, the soldiers are wearing laced shoes and leggings.

"With the lieutenant in the lead, a Soviet village is pacified," says the caption of a propaganda postcard from the "Officers in Battle" series. On this occasion the lieutenant wore wraparound leggings and laced shoes.

The overcoat remained closed for all ranks and proved to be of "peacetime quality" for the troops on the eastern front in the war's first winter. Following the saying, "it's better than nothing", the soldiers froze in it. Padded winter combat uniforms made up for this lack only as of 1943.

Right: General of the Infantry Friedrich Hossbach was one of the few generals to be decorated with the Army Medal of Honor; he wears it here on the ribbon of the Iron Cross second class. As can be seen, the Reichswehr jacket with set-in side pockets was worn by many generals until the end of World War II.

Above: Colonel Ivo-Thilo of the General Staff in 1944, wearing the combat jacket with open collar and gray shirt with black tie. Wearing the combat jacket with open collar was ordered on certain occasions and was customary for troops fighting at the front in the summer.

Right: Here too, the way of wearing the combat jacket with open collar by all ranks can be seen. The camouflage paint on the steel helmets is interesting. Just as in World War I, camouflage helmet paint was experimented with in the last years of World War II. The different results did not lead to a uniform regulation, and the use of such paint was to be decided by the unit commander and the material situation at the location. The First Lieutenant in the foreground wears the 43 field cap and a 43 combat jacket with a field-gray collar.

An infantry rifleman in overcoat and a black belt with box buckle worn outside it, plus woolen gloves.

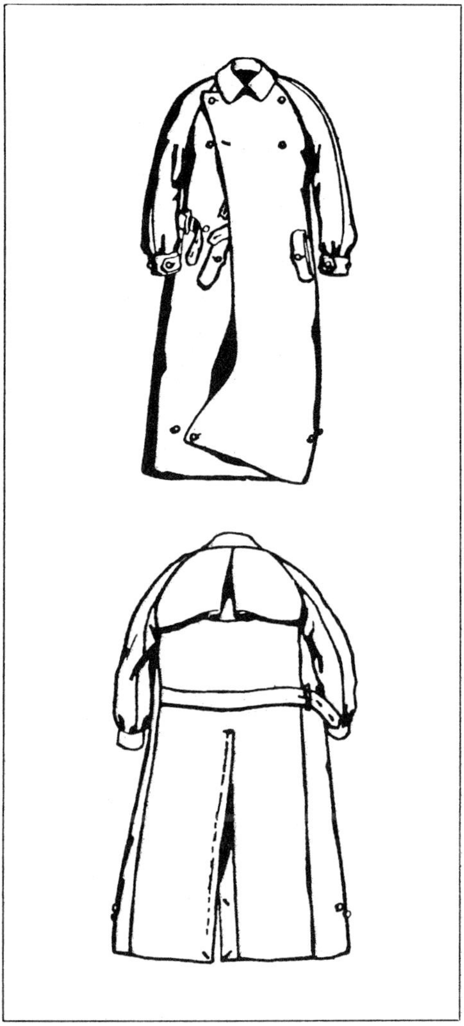

The motor vehicle drivers' protective coat (above and left) consisted of cloth-reinforced rubberized material. The lower part of the coat could be buttoned around the knees, thus providing cold-weather protection as well as leg freedom for motorcycle drivers. Buttoned-on shoulder patches and flaps were worn on the shoulders of the drivers' coat.

Above: Field-gray leather coat for army officers. The shoulder patches and flaps were always buttoned onto these coats.

Upper right: Generals left the top button unbuttoned so the red lapel lining was visible.

The same applied to wearers of the Knight's Cross, so they could show their decoration for great bravery.

Right: Senior General Heinrici, Commander of the Fourth Army, wears a coat with fur collar, which was allowed for officers.

Sport Clothes

Army sports clothing consisted of a white sport shirt with a black national emblem and dark brown sport trousers with a back pocket on one or the other side. In addition, triangular swimming trunks and sport shoes were issued. The official designation of the training clothing of dark blue knit went down in history as the "sport shooting suit." The two-part suit consisted of a jacket with an inside pocket on the left side and a zipper for closing. The trousers of the same material had no pockets. For special sporting activities there were colorful striped soccer and handball shirts.

The dark blue training suit was not usually equipped with the national emblem on the right breast side. On the other hand, a big woven national eagle on a white background was always worn on the sport shirt.

The Rifleman's Emblem

The rifleman's cord as a marksman's emblem had a tradition in the imperial German army that went back to 1894. By "All-Highest Cabinet Order" of January 27, 1894, the black-white-red rifleman's cord was introduced. The other German states followed this example. Until 1920, the rifleman's cord remained the typical shooting decoration for the infantry.

With the new Reichsheer uniform, the rifleman's cord was eliminated, and the old type of shooting decorations in the form of bars and patches on the sleeve came back into use. From the introduction of shooting decorations at the end of the Eighteenth Century, until the introduction of the rifleman's cord, this form of recognizing good shooting was customary in the infantry. The shooting decoration introduced in December of 1920, with ten classes and a sharpshooter class, consisted of 8-cm green or silver braid with woven-in green stripes. It was worn on the jacket, on the front of the left sleeve cuff (see p. 50).

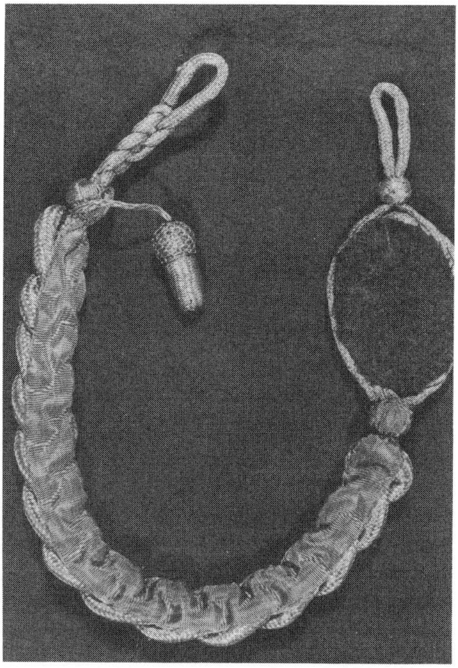

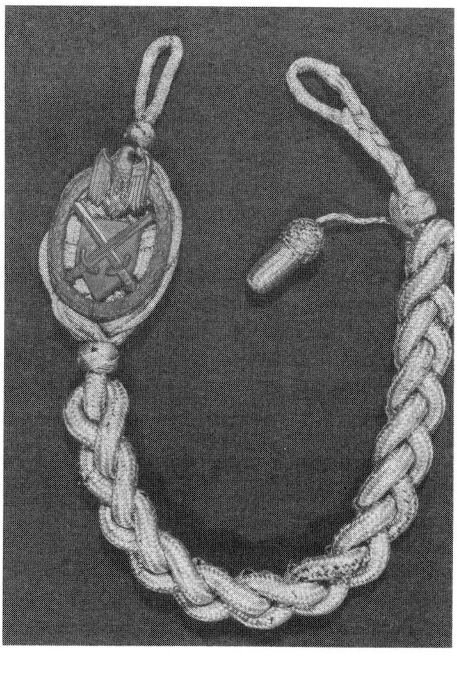

Riflemen's cords for the army, class two, recognizable by the shield with crossed swords (used in this form since 1939) and the acorn of aluminum thread. Above: On the back, the cord and the weave behind the shield were covered to protect the uniform.

It became obvious very soon that the division was no longer sufficient, and as of January 27, 1928 the classes were extended to 24.

In principle, decoration "for particularly achievements in school shooting with rifle, carbine, light and heavy machine gun and in mortar-firing and artillery service." The decoration was good for a year, and after new achievements the next higher grade could be granted.

The sharpshooter class was a special entity, given without class rank for appropriate achievement. The members of the sharpshooter class wore an eight-millimeter matt silver braid, with a brush at the bottom and a 1.5-mm green stripe in the middle under their shooting decoration at a distance of half a centimeter. In June of 1936 the rifleman's cord was re-introduced in the Wehrmacht army. The braided cord (8-mm aluminum thread) ended in a rosette of 3-mm cord to which the medal was attached.

Schützenabzeichen.

Die Schützenschnur wird von der rechten Schulter nach der Brust getragen und hier am zweiten Waffenrock- oder Feldblusenknopf befestigt. Sie ist eine Fangschnur aus mattem Aluminiumgespinst und wird getragen zum Parade-, Melde-, Ausgeh- und Wachanzug. Sie wird in 12 Stufen verliehen, und zwar:

Stufe	Auf der Rosette eine Plakette mit	Schieber	Anzahl der Eicheln	Für Artillerie: Anzahl der Granaten
1	Hoheitsabzeichen und Schild aus mattem Leichtmetall	aus mattem Aluminiumgespinst (Stufe 1–8)		
2	wie vor		1 } aus mattem Aluminiumgespinst	1 } wie vor
3	wie vor		2	2
4	wie vor		3	3
5	Hoheitsabzeichen und Schild mit 2 gekreuzten antiken Schwertern, umgeben von einem Eichenlaubkranz aus mattem Leichtmetall			
6	wie vor		1 } aus mattem Aluminiumgespinst	1 } wie vor
7	wie vor		2	2
8	wie vor		3	3
9	Hoheitsabzeichen und Schild mit 2 gekreuzten antiken Schwertern, umgeben von einem Eichenlaubkranz aus mattem, vergoldetem Leichtmetall	aus mattem Goldgespinst (Stufe 9–12)		
10	wie vor		1 } aus mattem Goldgespinst	1 } wie vor
11	wie vor		2	2
12	wie vor		3	3

How the rifleman's cord, second class, was worn since 1939.

Plaque for shooting decorations, classes 5 to 8, of antique silver-colored light metal, and antique gold-colored light metal for classes 9 to 12.

The rifleman's cord was given in twelve classes, with different plaques. Originally, the first to fourth classes had a simple shield of matt silver light metal with the national emblem. In January of 1939 the shield for these classes was given a smooth oak-leaf wreath and two crossed swords. Classes five to eight had a matt silver plaque with a raised oak-leaf wreath, and from the ninth class up the plaque was gold-colored. The class divisions were represented by the corresponding number of aluminum-thread acorns.

The shield of the rifleman's cord for the first to fourth classes, made of antique silver-colored light metal. These shields were worn from June of 1936 until the introduction of the new wreath in January of 1939.

The Infantry Assault Medal

Even in the 1939 Polish campaign, which lasted only six weeks, it had been seen that the Iron Cross alone was not a sufficient decoration for brave infantrymen. Recognizing this situation, the Commander of the Army, Senior General von Brauchitsch, ordered the creation of an infantry assault medal. After the evaluation of several designs submitted by the firm of C. E. Juncker of Berlin, the decoration came into being with the gun and fixed bayonet in an oak-leaf wreath, with the national eagle, as the symbol of the storming infantrymen. On December 20, 1939 the army commander signed the order, and the first medals were awarded in the French campaign. The awarding order read: "As a visible sign of recognition of the infantrymen who has proved himself in assault attack, but at the same time as an inducement to the highest fulfillment of duty, I hereby order the introduction of the Infantry Assault Medal for infantry rifle companies. The awarding of the Infantry Assault Medal will be carried out according to the enclosed criteria. I make the proper authorities responsible for upholding the criteria most exactly." In the OKH orders of May 1943 concerning medals, the criteria for conferring the Infantry Assault Medal were finally determined:

1. The Infantry Assault Medal can be awarded to officers, non-commissioned officers and men of grenadier regiments, motorized grenadier regiments, pursuit regiments (battalions), mountain pursuit regiments, which took part as of June 1, 1940 in a) three assault attacks, b) on the front line, c) penetrating with weapon in hand, d) on three different days of battle. Successful advances, countermoves and counterattacks are to be regarded as assault attacks as long as they led to close combat. Personal action in the defeat of enemy battle vehicles with close-combat weapons also qualifies

"A major recognizes the bravest with the EK II and the Infantry Assault Medal." Thus reads the caption of this postcard picture taken by a war wire-service reporter on January 31, 1942, passed on to the press as picture no. A 104059. The caption continues: "For 52 hours these soldiers from two Mecklenburg companies held off a Bolshevik division and were victorious in the battle."

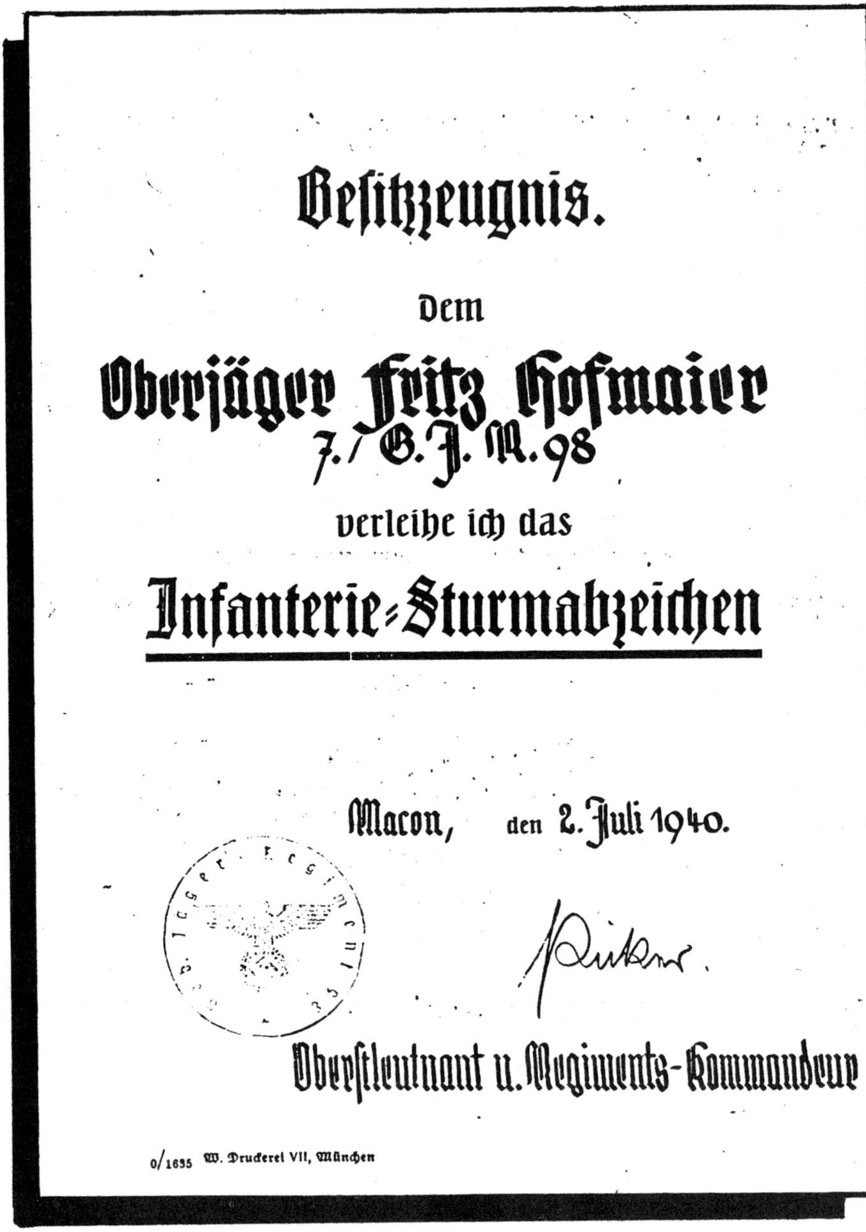

Besitzeugnis.

Dem

Oberjäger Fritz Hofmaier

7./G.J.R.98

verleihe ich das

Infanterie-Sturmabzeichen

Macon, den 2. Juli 1940.

Oberstleutnant u. Regiments-Kommandeur

0/1635 W. Druckerei VII, München

Only as of June 1940, after the creation of the Infantry Assault Medal in bronze, was a differentiation made between silver and bronze. Here is a certificate of award from the French campaign, in its "front form." (The recipient of the medal was Senior Pursuit Soldier Fritz Hofmaier).

The Infantry Assault Medal was one of the army's most frequently awarded decorations. Several hundred thousand of them were made and awarded. On account of the large numbers that were made, almost all manufacturers of medals produced Infantry Assault Medals. Above: the medal in silver, with a smooth back. This is what is called a massive construction. Below: the medal in bronze in its hollow, stamped form.

Inf. Regt. 8 (mot)

Besitzzeugnis

Dem

Schützen

Heinrich Leschner

10. / Inf. Regt. (mot) 8

verleihe ich das

Infanterie-Sturmabzeichen

in Bronze.

O. U., 22. Juli 1941.

Oberst u. Regt.-Kdr.

What with the numbers of Infantry Assault Medals awarded, the printers in Germany never caught up with the demand for official certificates. Down to regimental level, many of them were printed by the army, even at the front. (Certificate for Rifleman Heinrich Leschner.)

as assault attack. A recognition of assault attacks for the period from 1/1 to 5/31/1940 applies only to members of earlier rifle companies of non-motorized infantry divisions and mountain pursuit companies. For medical corpsmen, clause 1 c) is to be regarded as fulfilled when they, under the same conditions as the assaulting infantry, have cared for or protected wounded men in the close-combat area.

2. Members of grenadier, fusilier-pursuit and mountain pursuit regiments will be awarded the Infantry Assault Medal in silver, and members of motorized grenadier and fusilier regiments will be awarded the Infantry Assault Medal in bronze. The regimental commander is empowered to award the medals.

Lieutenant Hans-Olaf, Count von Sponeck is shown here wearing the classic "assortment of medals" of an infantryman. Along with the medals for bravery, the Iron Cross first and second class, are the Close Combat Badge in bronze as well as the Infantry Assault Medal and the wound medal, both in silver. He wears the Iron Cross second class in two forms, as a ribbon in his buttonhole and as a small medal ribbon under the Close Combat Badge. His 43 field cap with the insignia for the peaked cap is not exactly according to the rules.

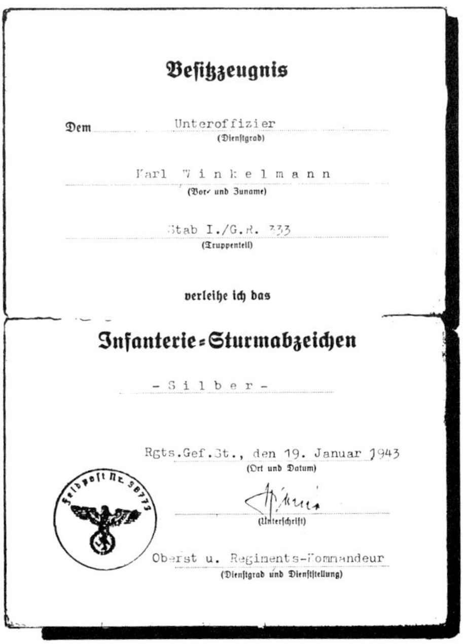

Besitzzeugnis

Dem Unteroffizier
(Dienstgrad)

Karl Winkelmann
(Vor- und Zuname)

Stab I./G.R. 333
(Truppenteil)

verleihe ich das

Infanterie-Sturmabzeichen

- Silber -

Rgts.Gef.St., den 19. Januar 1943
(Ort und Datum)

(Unterschrift)

Oberst u. Regiments-Kommandeur
(Dienstgrad und Dienststellung)

Left: Official printed form of the certificate of award for the Infantry Assault Medal, as it was usually given out during the war. (for Sergeant Karl Winkelmann.)

The Whites of the Enemy's Eyes

Only in the middle of the war, on November 25, 1942, did Adolf Hitler, in his role as supreme commander of the army, create the Close Combat Badge.

It was valued very highly by the soldiers, which was attributable to the fact that it was awarded only for officially recognized close combat days, and very strict standards were set. Thus it can be said that the awarding was "more just" than was the case with some other medals. And the fact that personal bravery in man-to-man combat was required also contributed.

Captain Traugott Kempas, Commander of the First Battalion of Grenadier Regiment 176, decorated with the Knight's Cross to the Iron Cross (awarded December 9, 1944) and the German Cross in Gold, as well as the silver Close Combat Badge and other battle decorations. As the 757th oak-leaf wearer in the Wehrmacht (awarded February 28, 1945), and at the rank of Major, Kampas fell in close combat on March 13, 1945 in the defense of a village near his birthplace on the East Prussian border.

For that reason, the Close Combat Badge was worn with special pride. The third level in particular, the golden Close Combat Badge, was regarded as the highest infantry decoration. The highest number of calculable close combat days has been set at eighty-four by Hermann Maringgele.

The orders reproduced here were amplified by appropriate directions.

On April 8, 1944 Adolf Hitler commanded (General Army Messages, No. 174) that he personally regarded the conferring of the golden Close Combat Badge as the highest infantry decoration. It was also stated that soldiers who had met the criteria for the golden Close Combat Badge have their names given to the OKH/PA by the appropriate regimental commanders through official channels. To maintain the high value of the Close Combat Badge, it was directed that particularly strict criteria be applied in determining the grade of the Close Combat Badge. On September 21, 1944 a further directive (General Army Messages, No. 443) followed. It stated that the Close Combat Badge could be awarded only for front service, thus for action against regular troops, whereas for action against bands (partisans were meant) the Band Combat Medal, established on

The Close Combat Badge was awarded at three levels (bronze, silver and gold).

January 30, 1944, was to be awarded. Thus action against partisans could no longer be considered for the awarding of the Close Combat Badge.

"The Three from the Sixth", is the caption under this postcard picture. War correspondent Knirsch took the picture on December 11, 1943. The text went on to say, "Company leader, non-commissioned officer and senior corporal, linked not only by friendship but also the silver Close Combat Badge, earned under the hardest conditions." The 43 field cap and the open collars of the 43 combat jacket with field-gray collars for non-commissioned officers and men are easy to recognize here.

Auszüge der Verordnungstexte

a) Verordnung
über die Stiftung der Nahkampfspange
vom 25. November 1942

Als sichtbares Zeichen der Anerkennung des mit der blanken Waffe und Nahkampfmitteln Mann gegen Mann kämpfenden Soldaten, zugleich aber auch als Ansporn zu höchster Pflichterfüllung stifte ich die

Nahkampfspange.

Die Verleihung der Nahkampfspange ist nach beifolgenden Bestimmungen durchzuführen. Für die genaueste Einhaltung der Bestimmungen sind die zuständigen Vorgesetzten verantwortlich.

Führerhauptquartier, den 25. November 1942

Der Führer und Oberbefehlshaber des Heeres
Adolf Hitler

b) Bestimmungen

zur Verordnung über die Stiftung der Nahkampfspange vom 25. November 1942

1. Die Nahkampfspange wird als Anerkennung dem Soldaten verliehen, der sich vielfach im Nahkampf „Mann gegen Mann" mit der Waffe in der Hand seiner Aufgabe entsprechend bewährt hat.

Das Infanteriesturmabzeichen bleibt unabhängig hiervon mit den zu dessen Erwerb geforderten besonderen Bedingungen bestehen.

2. Die Nahkampfspange wird in 3 Stufen verliehen und auf der linken Seite 1 cm über der Ordensschnalle getragen. Bei Erwerb einer höheren Stufe ist die vorhergehende abzulegen. Sie bleibt jedoch im Besitz des Inhabers.

3. Die Bedingungen für die Verleihungen sind:

Für die 1. Stufe	(Bronze)	15	Nahkämpfe
„ „ 2. „	(Silber)	30	„
„ „ 3. „	(Gold)	50	„

4. Als Nahkampftage sind anzurechnen:

a) Alle Kampftage, an denen die auszuzeichnenden Kämpfer Gelegenheit fanden, „das Weiße im Auge des Feindes" zu sehen, d. h. mit Nahkampfwaffen mit dem Gegner Mann gegen Mann im Kampf bis zur letzten Entscheidung zu stehen.

b) Dieses kann also im Großangriff, beim Spähtruppgang, in der Abwehr, bei einem einzelnen Meldegang, bei einem feindlichen Spähtruppunternehmen usw. gegeben sein.

c) Der Ort — bei den Gefechtsvorposten, im Vorfeld, in der HKL., in der Artillerie-Feuerstellung, im rückwärtigen Heeresgebiet (z. B. Partisanenkampf) oder beim Überfall auf einen Lazarettzug oder eine Versorgungskolonne — spielt dabei gar keine Rolle.

5. Jeder Soldat, der ungeschützt und zu Fuß in eine unter Ziff. 4 geschilderte Lage kommt und sich hier bewährt, hat die Anwartschaft auf die Spange.

6. a) Auf Vorschlag der Kp.Führer, der unverzüglich — möglichst noch am gleichen Tage mit der Tagesmeldung — abzugeben ist, legen die Kommandeure der Regimenter, selbständigen Batle. usw. im Tagesbefehl den anzurechnenden Nahkampftag für die beteiligten Einheiten fest.

7. Jeder Mann hat im Soldbuch ein Blatt (Muster 2,) bei sich zu tragen, in dem der anzurechnende Nahkampftag einzutragen und zu bescheinigen ist.

Für die Führer vom Kp.Führer an aufwärts ist der Nahkampftag durch den nächsthöheren, für den jeweiligen Einsatz zuständigen Vorgesetzten zu bescheinigen und entsprechende Zweitschrift bei den Pers.Papieren zu führen.

8. a) Die Nahkampftage sind ab 1. 12. 1942 anzurechnen.

b) Um den vielfach bewährten alten Frontkämpfer hervorzuheben, können jedoch bei ununterbrochenem Einsatz im Osten[1]) nach dem 22. 6. 1941[2])

von 15 Monaten	bis zu 15	Nahkampftage
„ 12 „	„ „ 10	„
„ 8 „	„ „ 5	„

nach durch gewissenhafte Prüfung des Einheitsführers geführtem Nachweis angerechnet werden.

c) Der Div.Kdr. kann an Soldaten, für die durch schwere Verwundung in Zukunft keine Gelegenheit zum Nahkampf mehr gegeben ist, die Nahkampfspange verleihen[3]).

Hierzu muß der zu Beleihende für den Erwerb

der 1. Stufe	mindestens 10	Nahkampftage
„ 2. „	„ 20	„
„ 3. „	„ 40	„

nachweisen.

Über die Anrechnung von Nahkampftagen vor dem 1. 12. 1942 siehe unter b).

9. a) An Gefallene, Verstorbene und tödlich Verunglückte ist die Nahkampfspange gegebenenfalls nachträglich zu verleihen, wenn sie vor dem Tode oder mit dem Tage ihres Todes die Bedingungen erfüllten. Die verliehene Auszeichnung ist mit Besitzurkunde den Hinterbliebenen als Erinnerungsstück zu übersenden.

b) In Kriegsgefangenschaft geratene oder vermißte Soldaten verlieren den Anspruch auf die Nahkampfspange.

10. Der Kp.- usw. Führer beantragt die Verleihung der in Frage kommenden Stufe der Nahkampfspange beim verleihungsberechtigten Rgt.- bzw. selbst. Btl.- oder Abt.-Kommandeur (Muster 3,).

Über die Verleihung der Nahkampfspange sind von den verleihenden Kommandeuren Besitzzeugnisse (Muster 4,) auszustellen. Nur diese berechtigen zum Tragen der Nahkampfspange

See page 127 for English translation.

On the same date, (General Army Messages, No. 511), a further order was given as to the recognition of wearers of the golden Close Combat Badge, as Hitler in (his) first awarding of the golden Close Combat Badge had ascertained that a non-commissioned officer to whom he awarded the golden Close Combat Badge was not yet in possession of the Iron Cross first class.

He made up for this on the spot by awarding the non-commissioned officer the Iron Cross first class personally.

Thereupon it was ordered that in the future it was to be ascertained whether the soldiers who had proved their readiness to participate and their bravery in numerous close combats were not already eligible for the Iron Cross first class.

BESITZZEUGNIS

DEM Revieroberwachtmeister der Schutzpolizei
(DIENSTGRAD)

August Göpfert
(VOR- UND FAMILIENNAME)

II./ -Polizei - Gebirgsjäger - Regiment 18
(TRUPPENTEIL)

VERLEIHE ICH FÜR TAPFERE TEILNAHME
AN 15 NAHKAMPFTAGEN

DIE 1. STUFE DER
NAHKAMPFSPANGE

Rgts.Gef.Std., den 22.12.44
(ORT UND DATUM)

(UNTERSCHRIFT)

Major und Regiments - Führer
(DIENSTGRAD UND DIENSTSTELLUNG)

The most frequent form of certificate for the Close Combat Badges was printed and had a DIN A5 format.

A soldier in close combat throwing a hand grenade. The helmets have been smeared with loam and soil to match the color of the ground.

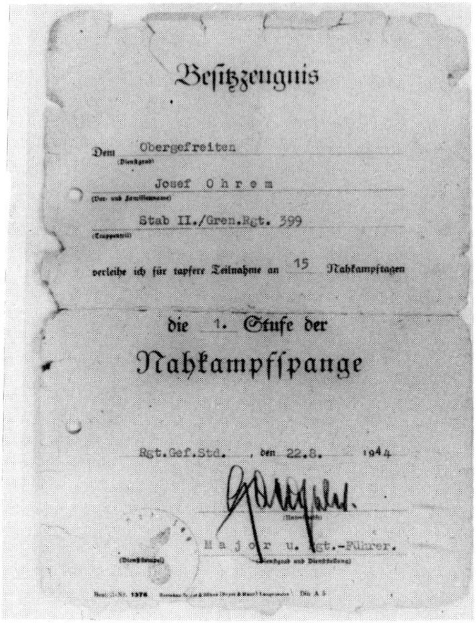

Besitzzeugnis

Dem Obergefreiten
(Dienstgrad)

Josef Ohrem
(Vor- und Familienname)

Stab II./Gren.Rgt. 399
(Truppenteil)

verleihe ich für tapfere Teilnahme an 15 Nahkampftagen

die 1. Stufe der

Nahkampfspange

Rgt.Gef.Std., den 22.8. 1944

Major u. Rgt.-Führer.

On these two pages various forms of the certificate of possession of the Close Combat Badge with different types of script are shown.

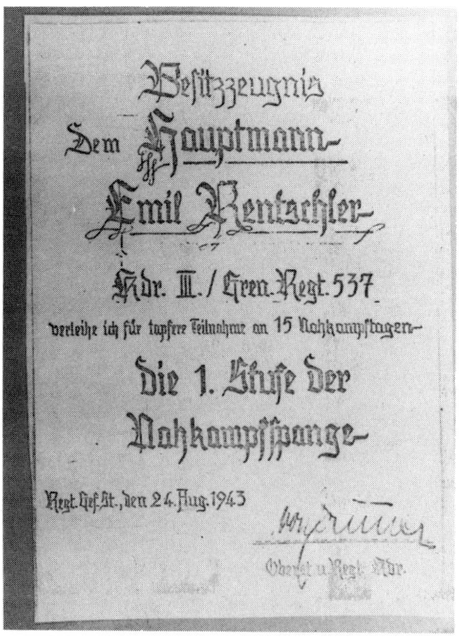

Besitzzeugnis

Dem Hauptmann

Emil Rentschler

Kdr. II./Gren.Regt.537

verleihe ich für tapfere Teilnahme an 15 Nahkampftagen

die 1. Stufe der

Nahkampfspange

Regt.Gef.St., den 24.Aug.1943

Oberst u. Regt.-Kdr.

It was recommended that this check be made with the awarding of the silver Close combat Badge at the latest. When awarding the highest level of the Close Combat Badge, it should be ascertained whether the criteria for awarding the German Cross in gold had been met. Since the number of fifty close combat days represented a very special achievement, this was accepted as self-evident. Adolf Hitler agreed that wearers of the golden Close Combat Badge should be submitted for awarding of the German Cross in gold with further conditions.

A further extension of the criteria was made on November 4, 1944, according to which so-called back-fighters, meaning soldiers who had been separated from their troop and fought their way back to their unit (back-fought) should receive the next higher level of the decorations that they already held. This also applied to the Close Combat Badge.

How many Close Combat Badges of the various levels were awarded can no longer be determined and probably will never again be provable. But it can be said that the Close Combat Badge in bronze was awarded relatively frequently. But even in the case of the silver Close Combat Badge, a clear decrease in the number of awards can be determined. As for the highest level, the Close Combat Badge in gold, the rarity of its awarding could make a more exact determination possible.

Since only 403 wearers of the golden Close Combat Badge (army, Luftwaffe field units and Waffen-SS) had been reported to the OKH/Section P5 by the end of April 1945, it was long assumed that the number of awards was below 500. Thanks to intensive

Muster 4 zu Nr. 1030
AHM. 1342

Besitz-Zeugnis

Dem

Feldwebel
(Dienstgrad)

Fritz Werner
(Vor- und Familienname)

2./Panzergrenadier Regiment 8 (gp)
(Truppenteil)

verleihe ich für tapfere Teilnahme an 30 Nahkampftagen

die 2. Stufe der Nahkampfspange

O.U., den 20.4.44
(Ort und Datum)

[signature]
(Unterschrift)

Oberst u. Rgt.Kdr.
(Dienstgrad und -stellung)

5124 Gustav Kühn, Neuruppin

research, the number of golden Close Combat Badges awarded could now be determined fairly exactly. According to the present state of research, the number is 584, including three badges awarded to Luftwaffe personnel.

On August 27, 1944 Hitler awarded the golden Close Combat Badge to fourteen men of the army and the Waffen-SS. This was mentioned in the army reports with the words: "The Führer has, in the first awarding of the gold Close Combat Badge . . ." so that it is generally assumed that the first awarding of the golden Close Combat Badge took place on this day. Press reports also mention this, although with the words: "The Führer received at his headquarters fourteen soldiers of the army and the Waffen-SS to whom, as the first members of the German Wehrmacht, the golden Close Combat Badge was recently awarded. The Führer personally gave these soldiers the high decoration that, like no other, represents personal action

Sergeant Friedrich Billau was awarded the Close Combat Badge in gold on October 26, 1943 (the photo was taken on that day). It was actually given to him only on September 5, 1944, by Hitler personally. Until then he wore a gold-colored badge of the type and quality of other badges.

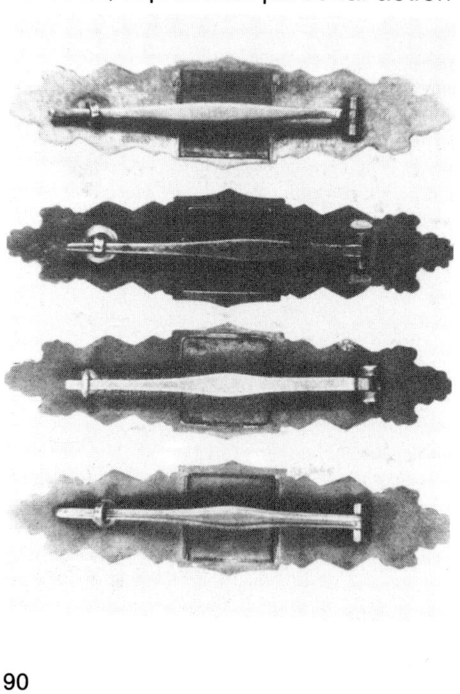

Left: The Close Combat Badges were made of tombac alloy, later of fine zinc, and then bronzed (very light to very dark shades exist) or silvered and polished as well as gilded and polished. The inset square metal plate was made of sheet steel (magnetic) and colored black to steel gray. Here are the backs of various badges with the existing types of pins, hooks and bars.

in more than 50 days of close combat." From the press reports it can thus be assumed that the awarding of these 14 golden Close Combat Badges had already taken place before August 27, and that Hitler had only acted out the awarding. This press release also gave rise to the error that these 14 awardings of the golden Close Combat Badge had been the first awardings of this level ever. It is nevertheless provable through documents that the highest level of Close Combat Badge had been awarded before this date. The first documentable award took place on August 10, 1943, to Hans Juchem. About a year, then, before the previously accepted date.

The assumption that the awarding of golden Close Combat Badges was always made by Hitler personally is also incorrect. He had in fact (as

Colonel Heinrich Volker, as chief of the staff company of Armored Grenadier Regiment 73, received the Knight's Cross on January 19, 1943, and was honored with the Close Combat Badge in gold in December of 1944.

Abschrift.

FS vom 15.12.44

(Träger der goldenen Nahkampfspange. Auf Befehl des Führers 1 Jahr Schule).

An
Wehrkreiskommando XI
pp.

Mit Wirkung vom 18.12.44 wird versetzt:
Major V o l k e r , Heinrich, Kdr.Pz.Gren.Rgt.119 der 25.Pz.Gren.Div., RDA: 1.8.43(661) Pz.Gren.Rgt.73, geb. [illegible], in die Pz.Tr.Schule Bergen zur Verwendung als Leiter Btl.Fhr.-Lehrgang.
Beorderung durch 25.Pz.Gren.Div.
Inmarschsetzung nach Bergen.

OKH/PA Ag P1/3.Abt.(a)
I.A.gez. Bachelin,Gen.Maj.u.Ag.-Chef

- - - - - - - - - -

Stellv.Generalkommando XI.A.K.
(Wehrkreiskommando XI)
Abt. IIa1 Az. Schule

Hannover, den 28.12.44.
H. / App. 2338

Abschrift.

Zusatz: Maj. Volker ist bis 2.1.45 beurlaubt.

Für das stellv.Generalkommando
Der Chef des Stabes
I.A.

Verteiler:
Herrn Maj.Volker,Barsinghausen/Deister
Pz.Tr.Schule Bergen

Directly linked with the awarding of the Close Combat Badge in gold was the transfer to a school unit. The "old foxes" were to pass their knowledge on to the young fellows. (The order transfers Heinrich Volker to Instructional Area Command XI, to lead a battalion at the Armored Training School in Bergen.)

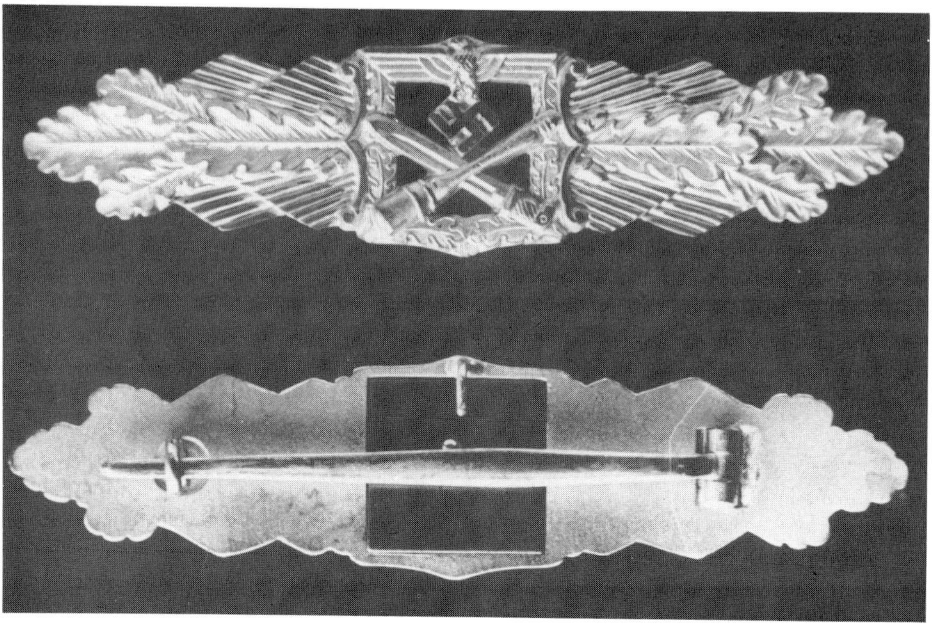

Front and back of the Close Combat Badge in gold, awarded to Karl Winkelmann on November 27, 1944 (see certificate at right). The hooks over the iron plate and the rivet that holds the plate to the badge are typical.

mentioned) reserved this for himself, but in practice it was done somewhat differently. The golden Close Combat Badges awarded before the order, which could only have been a very small number, were awarded and handed out by the appropriate commanders. But after the order too (April 1944), the golden Close Combat Badge was not always awarded by Hitler.

1.) On August 27, 1944, to 14 soldiers, by Adolf Hitler at the Führer's Headquarters.

2.) On September 5, 1944, to 14 soldiers, by Adolf Hitler at the Führer's Headquarters.

3.) On September 14, 1944, to nine soldiers, by Adolf Hitler at the Führer's Headquarters.

4.) On September 26, 1944, to 13 soldiers, by Adolf Hitler at the Führer's Headquarters.

5.) On October 23, 1944, to seven soldiers, by Heinrich Himmler (in his capacity as commander of the replacement army) at the Führer's Headquarters.

6.) On December 12, 1944, to 81 or 83 soldiers by Heinrich Himmler at the City Hall in Ulm (the medal was given to 81 soldiers during the official ceremonies, and to two soldiers, who had arrived late, during the subsequent dinner).

7.) On February 16, 1945, to 16 soldiers, by Heinrich Himmler in Bernau.

8.) On March 10, 1945, to 13 soldiers, by Senior General Heinz Guderian (in his capacity as Chief of the Army General Staff) at the OKH command post in Zossen.

Single awards:

1.) On September 14, 1944, to Leon Degrelle, by Adolf Hitler at the Führer's Headquarters, along with the oak leaves for the Knight's Cross of the Iron Cross.

2.) On February 20, 1945, to Hermann

Maringgele and Joachim Boosfeld, by Adolf Hitler at the Führer's Headquarters.

Along with the awarding of the highest level went a special 21-day furlough. In addition, the holders of the golden Close Combat Badge were to pass on their experience in close combat to young soldiers back home. To the extent that this was possible, the wearers of the Close Combat Badge in gold were transferred to schools or training units. In addition, they received the same special treatment by army procurement officers as did the wearers of the Knight's Cross. The manufacture of the Close Combat Badge was done according to a design by the painter and graphic artist Wilhelm Peekhaus of Berlin, by the firms of: Arbeitsgemeinschaft Metall und Kunststoff in Gablonz (trade mark: A. G. M. u. K. Gablonz),—C. E., Juncker in Berlin (name written out),—Friedrich Linden in Lüdenscheid (trade mark: FLL),—Funcke & Brüninghaus in Lüdenscheid (trade mark: F & BL),—Hymmen & Co. in Lüdenscheid (trade mark: H & C L and L/53),—Gebr. Wegerhoff in Lüdenscheid (trade mark: GWL in a circle), and—Rudolf Souval in Vienna (trade mark: R.S.). The trade mark appeared on the back of the badge.

Cavalry Captain Günther Konopacki received the golden Close Combat Badge as Commander of the Reconnaissance Instruction Section.

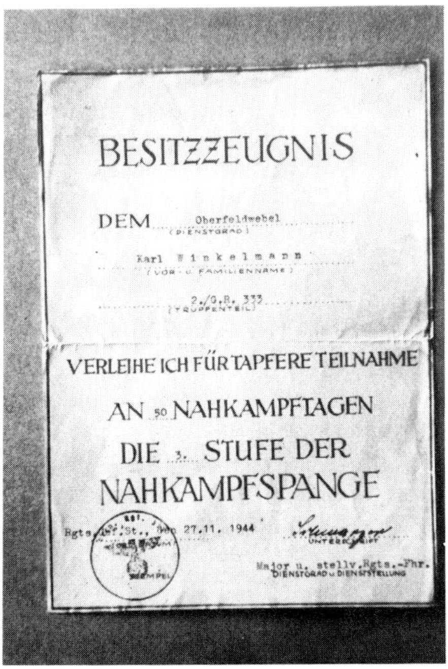

BESITZZEUGNIS

DEM Oberfeldwebel
(DIENSTGRAD)

Karl Winkelmann
(VOR- u. FAMILIENNAME)

2./G.R. 333
(TRUPPENTEIL)

VERLEIHE ICH FÜR TAPFERE TEILNAHME

AN 50 NAHKAMPFTAGEN

DIE 3. STUFE DER

NAHKAMPFSPANGE

Rgts.Gef.St., den 27.11.1944

UNTERSCHRIFT

Major u. stellv.Rgts.-Fhr.
DIENSTGRAD u. DIENSTSTELLUNG

The Sharpshooter's Insignia

The "sharpshooters' shootout" at the bridgehead on the Liza, the northernmost theater of war on the Arctic front from 1941 to 1945, is often mentioned in historic studies. Frozen fronts with little battle activity were the ideal situation for the Russian and German sharpshooters. A sharpshooters' battle for the company support base of the 2nd Battalion of the 143rd Mountain Regiment was described by Major Hellmut Raithel, a holder of the Knight's Cross: "Within a few hours, one mountain soldier fell with a bullet in his head and another had a bullet nick his ear. I ran to the front of the position. 'Bobinger, show now what you can do with your sharpshooters.' There is only one answer to enemy sharpshooters—namely, even better sharpshooters. The next day's evening report included eleven enemies shot by Bobinger and his

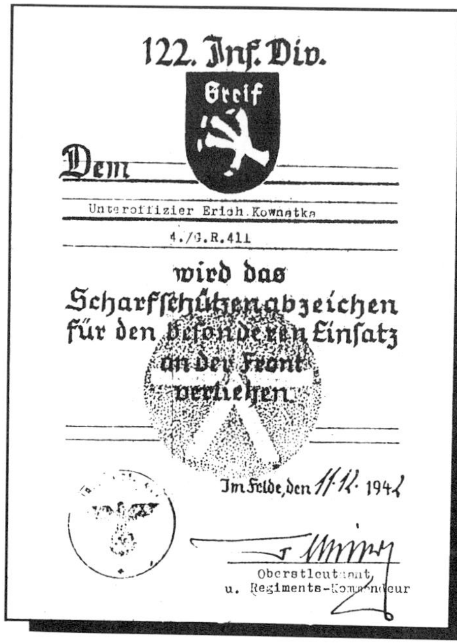

122. Inf. Div.

Greif

Dem

Unteroffizier Erich Kownatka

4./G.R.411

wird das Scharfschützenabzeichen für den besonderen Einsatz an der Front verliehen

Im Felde, den 11.12. 1942

Oberstleutnant u. Regiments-Kommandeur

Above: Before the official introduction of the sharpshooter's emblem, there were various emblems and certificates that were used independently by divisions. The need to recognize the achievement was felt more strongly at the front than in the "planning" sections, which disagreed with each other for a very long time about the establishment of a sharpshooter's emblem.

Left: A German sharpshooter in action.

men; one day later it was almost that many. After three times 24 hours the Russians knew once again who dominated the altitude of 314.8 meters. Oberjäger Hans Bobinger was victorious in a sharpshooting fight for the 25th time. I did not tell anyone that I had recommended Hans for the Iron Cross first class. I gave it to him the next day." The Iron Cross was the usual decoration for sharpshooters until the end of August 1944.

Dated August 20, 1944 a "Führer's Order" came from the "Führer and Supreme Commander of the Wehrmacht, Adolf Hitler", instituting the sharpshooter's emblem. The order stated:

1. To recognize the high utilization of the single shooter with a rifle as a sharpshooter, and to attest to the success thus achieved, I am instituting the sharpshooter's insignia for the army and the Waffen-SS. The emblem will be given at three levels.

2. The guidelines for carrying this out are assigned by the General of the Infantry to the Chief of the General Staff of the Army. Simultaneously with

An official drawing from the naval regulation sheet, portraying the second and third levels of the sharpshooter's emblem very clearly. After World War II the emblem was copied many times. It must be said that the copiers did not follow this pattern very closely, although it corresponds to the original. Thus copies can be identified easily by comparison with the original on page 97.

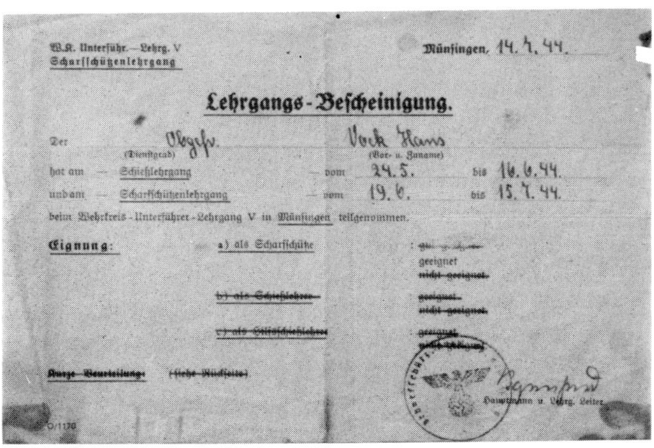

W.K. Unterführ.—Lehrg. V
Scharfschützenlehrgang

Münsingen, 14. 7. 44.

Lehrgangs-Bescheinigung.

Der Obgefr. (Dienstgrad) Vock Hans (Vor- u. Zuname)

hat am — Schießlehrgang — vom 24.5. bis 16.6.44.

und am — Scharfschützenlehrgang — vom 19.6. bis 15.7.44.

beim Wehrkreis-Unterführer-Lehrgang V in Münsingen teilgenommen.

Eignung: a) als Scharfschütze: geeignet

Hauptmann u. Lehrg. Leiter

D/1170

According to the regulations, only trained sharpshooters should be awarded the emblem. It does not seem very realistic that this stipulation was held to. Here is the training certificate of Senior Corporal Hans Vock for his successful sharpshooting training.

the publication of the Führer's order came the notification of the guidelines: The Führer had instituted a sharpshooter's emblem for the army and the SS troops. Thus the high utilization of the marksman with his rifle and his success in aimed individual shooting were to be recognized and, at the same time, an impetus was to be given for an increase in what had been achieved up to then. Accordingly, the sharpshooter's emblem was to be awarded according to the following principles:

1. The sharpshooter's emblem will be awarded by the nearest superior troop officer, with the approval of a regimental commander at least, upon the written suggestion of the unit leader,

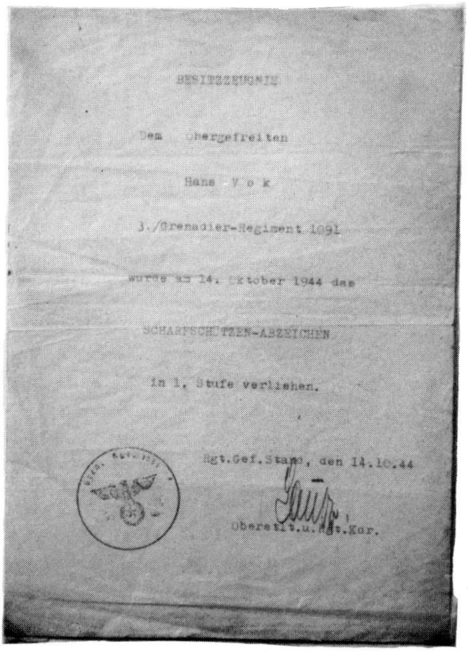

BESITZZEUGNIS

Dem Obergefreiten

Hans Vok

3./Grenadier-Regiment 1091

wurde am 14. Oktober 1944 das

SCHARFSCHÜTZEN-ABZEICHEN

in 1. Stufe verliehen.

Rgt.Gef.Stand, den 14.10.44

Oberstlt.u.Rgt.Kdr.

Printed certificates of possession of the sharpshooter's emblem have not yet been found. Typewritten certificates following the official model were made out at the front.

547.

DEM

Obergefreiten Hans Vock

SPRECHE ICH FÜR

30 bestätigte

Scharfschützenabschüsse

in der Zeit vom 10.8.-11.10.1944

MEINE BESONDERE

ANERKENNUNG

AUS

DIV.-GEFECHTSSTAND, DEN 14. Oktober 1944

GENERALMAJOR U. DIV.-KDR.

Simultaneously with the awarding of the sharpshooter's emblem first class (below), Senior Corporal Hans Vock received this certificate of recognition from his division.

to such soldiers who have been trained and utilized as sharpshooters according to plan. A certificate of award is to be given to the recipient, and the award is to be recorded in his personal papers.

2. The emblem is divided into three classes and worn on the lower right arm. Insofar as a soldier possesses a functional insignia of rank or is accorded one in addition to the sharpshooter's emblem, this is to be worn under the sharpshooter's emblem.

3. Awarded will be: The first class for at least 20 enemies shot, these to be scored after September 1, 1944 (emblem without special border), the second class for at least 40 enemies

On December 16, 1944 Senior Corporal Heinrich Franken of the 7th Company of Grenadier Regiment 58 received the third-level sharpshooter's emblem. His original emblem is shown at the right. The emblem, 4.5 cm wide and 6 cm high, is bordered with a 2.5-mm cellon cord. The machine-embroidered emblems were worn on the lower right sleeve of the combat jacket.

shot, scored after September 1, 1944 (emblem with silver cord border), the third class for at least sixty enemies shot, scored after September 1, 1944 (emblem with gold cord border). Shooting in close combat will not be counted. In addition, the enemy must have been shot to immobility and may not have shown the intention of fleeing or surrendering.

4. Every successful shooting is to be reported to the unit and attested to by at least one witness. The units will make lists of sharpshooters for the purpose of these reports. An excerpt from the sharpshooters' list is to be turned over to the new unit along with the other papers in case of transfer.

A retroactive reckoning of shootings was not allowed, so as to avoid unnecessary paperwork. Rather it was suggested that previous achievements be recognized by the troop by awarding the Iron Cross.

OKH, 8/20/1944, General of the Infantry and Chief of the General Staff of the Army.

The awarding of the emblem exclusively to members of the army and Waffen-SS was changed at the beginning of 1945. According to Hitler's wishes, all soldiers who would be used in infantry fighting in the future could be awarded the sharpshooter's emblem. The Luftwaffe and navy thereupon established additional guidelines to regulate awards in their areas.

According to the guidelines for awarding and the additions to them, the certificate of award was to be made up by the awarding authorities on their own. This led, toward the end of the war, to the use of simple typewritten certificates, which simply had to follow the prescribed textual form: "Certificate of award. To . . . was awarded on . . . the sharpshooter's emblem of the . . . level." The official seal and the signature, rank and position of the awarding commander

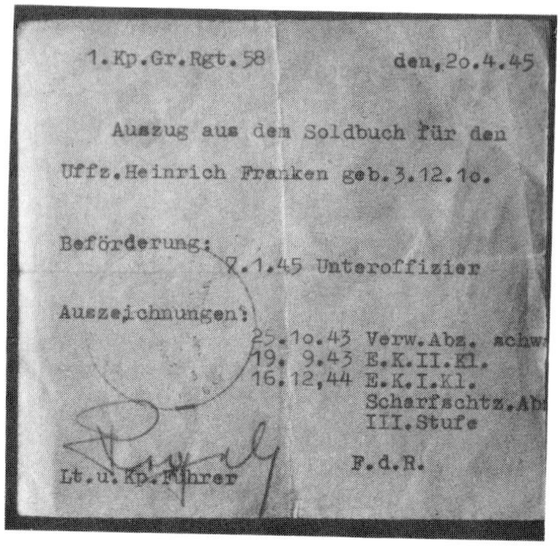
1.Kp.Gr.Rgt.58 den,20.4.45

Auszug aus dem Soldbuch für den

Uffz.Heinrich Franken geb.3.12.10.

Beförderung:
1.1.45 Unteroffizier

Auszeichnungen:
25.10.43 Verw.Abz. schw
19. 9.43 E.K.II.Kl.
16.12,44 E.K.I.Kl.
Scharfschtz.Ab
III.Stufe

Lt.u.Kp.Führer F.d.R.

The page added to the salary book of sergeant Heinrich Franken attesting to his sharpshooter's emblem, third level.

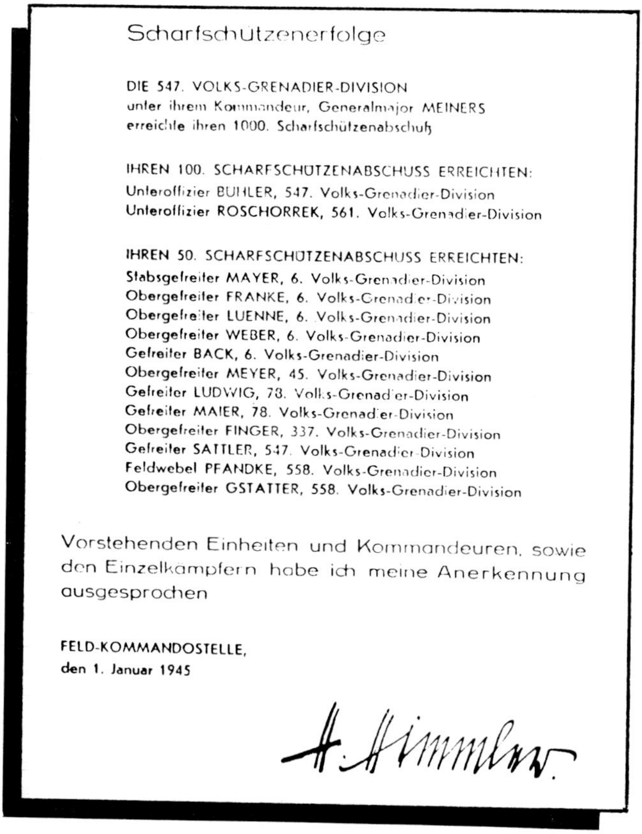
Scharfschützenerfolge

DIE 547. VOLKS-GRENADIER-DIVISION
unter ihrem Kommandeur, Generalmajor MEINERS
erreichte ihren 1000. Scharfschützenabschuß

IHREN 100. SCHARFSCHÜTZENABSCHUSS ERREICHTEN:
Unteroffizier BÜHLER, 547. Volks-Grenadier-Division
Unteroffizier ROSCHORREK, 561. Volks-Grenadier-Division

IHREN 50. SCHARFSCHÜTZENABSCHUSS ERREICHTEN:
Stabsgefreiter MAYER, 6. Volks-Grenadier-Division
Obergefreiter FRANKE, 6. Volks-Grenadier-Division
Obergefreiter LUENNE, 6. Volks-Grenadier-Division
Obergefreiter WEBER, 6. Volks-Grenadier-Division
Gefreiter BACK, 6. Volks-Grenadier-Division
Obergefreiter MEYER, 45. Volks-Grenadier-Division
Gefreiter LUDWIG, 78. Volks-Grenadier-Division
Gefreiter MAIER, 78. Volks-Grenadier-Division
Obergefreiter FINGER, 337. Volks-Grenadier-Division
Gefreiter SATTLER, 547. Volks-Grenadier-Division
Feldwebel PFANDKE, 558. Volks-Grenadier-Division
Obergefreiter GSTATTER, 558. Volks-Grenadier-Division

Vorstehenden Einheiten und Kommandeuren, sowie den Einzelkämpfern habe ich meine Anerkennung ausgesprochen

FELD-KOMMANDOSTELLE,
den 1. Januar 1945

H. Himmler

In his capacity as commander of the replacement army, Himmler encouraged the sharpshooters very much and particularly recognized successful sharpshooters (photo at right). He also gave gifts, such as a wristwatch and a special furlough for 50 shootings. For 100 shootings he gave a hunting rifle, a pistol or binoculars. The sharpshooters' attainments were published in special lists (an excerpt at left).

also belonged on the certificate. To be recorded on the application for awarding were, along with the sharpshooter's name and birthday, the place and day of the shootings, number of shootings, distances and witnesses. In addition, under a dividing line there were to be comments in brief form supporting the award by stating that the enemy was killed or left unable to move. This offers an idea of the criteria by which the emblem was awarded.

According to the law on titles, orders and medals in the Federal Republic of Germany of July 26, 1957, the levels of the sharpshooter's emblem are again allowed to be worn. Since the emblems do not show a swastika, they can also be produced legally to this day, and thus those found in collections and on the collectors' market are almost exclusively of postwar manufacture. Original emblems are extremely rare and correspondingly expensive.

Sie vernichteten zwei bolschewistische Kompanien.
Reichsführer SS Heinrich Himmler überreichte an besonders erfolgreiche Scharfschützen das Scharfschützenabzeichen.

They wiped out two Bolshevik companies.
Reichsführer Heinrich Himmler awards the sharpshooter's emblem to particularly successful sharpshooters.

Reich Grenadier Division "Hoch- und Deutschmeister"

The masters of the Order of Teutonic Knights called themselves Hoch- und Deutschmeister (High and German Masters) when the offices of the High Master and the German Master were united in one person. The title came into being after the transfer of the order's headquarters from Königsberg to Mergentheim in 1526. Archduke Maximilian of Austria (1589-1618) was the first to bear the combined title. The Peace of Pressburg of December 6, 1805 conveyed this hereditary office to the imperial house of Austria, an archduke of which always held it.

Shoulder patch of a lieutenant colonel of the Hoch- und Deutschmeister Reich Grenadier Division, with the added Deutschmeister Cross.

From then on the Austrian Infantry Regiment No. 4 bore the title of "Hoch- und Deutschmeister." The name was meant to indicate that the recruiting area of the regiment was in the imperial territories of the Teutonic Knights. Thus the Hoch- und Deutschmeister was originally not an Austrian regiment, but a German one from the Empire.

In April of 1938 the 44th Infantry Division was established in Vienna. With Regiments 131, 132 and 134, this division fought in Poland, France and Russia until the total defeat at Stalingrad in 1942-43.

After its reestablishment in March of 1943, when it was formed of Grenadier Regiments 887 and 888, the 44th Infantry Division was given the name "Reich Grenadier Division Hoch- und Deutschmeister" on June 3, 1943, and Grenadier Regiment 134, as the Viennese house regiment, was given the name "Reich Grenadier Regiment Hoch- und Deutschmeister."

Until the war ended, the Hoch- und Deutschmeister fought in Italy and Hungary. By order of March 23, 1944, members of this division's staff wore on their shoulder patches the modified "Deutschmeister Cross", also known as the "Stalingrad Cross", made of metal. According to an order of February 26, 1945, all soldiers of the division and the regiment were to wear a "Hoch- und Deutschmeister" armband, but this was never distributed. The shoulder-patch pin, on the other hand, was worn by all ranks in the division despite orders to the contrary. The hollow stamped cross of light metal measured 33 by 29 mm. This emblem called particular attention to the achievements and successes of the division. It ranked among the elite infantry divisions of the army.

The Deutschmeister Cross with its "extension", forming the so-called Stalingrad Cross.

Uniforms at the End of World War II

Combat uniforms had to correspond to the most varied weather conditions of the theaters of war and the troops' experiences in battle. Only after bitter experience was a special winter uniform introduced in the army. It came in two pieces, consisting of jacket and trousers with attached suspenders. Worn over the combat uniform, it not only offered protection from the weather but also against being sighted by the enemy. As a camouflage suit, it could be used in two ways: white for winter landscapes and, when turned inside out, mottled green and brown for snow-free country. Since the enemy also fought

A camouflage suit, which could be turned inside out and worn either as camouflage or as white winter camouflage.

The camouflage pattern of the army's triangular tent sections, also used for combat uniforms of camouflage material.

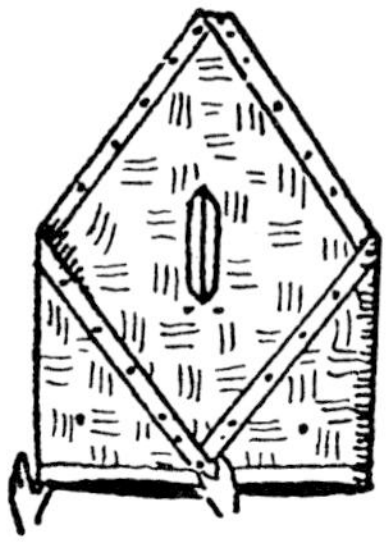

When the triangular tent section was to be used as a raincoat, one put one's head through the slit, and the piece fell with its long side to the back and the triangle points forward, where they were buttoned together.

in white camouflage clothing, colored recognition stripes had to be worn on the upper sleeves. The color of these stripes was changed daily according to a code that was given out. Pure camouflage suits cut like the 1943 combat uniform were an exception in the infantry and were worn chiefly by officers. Since the camouflage suits had no shoulder patches as a rule, special insignia of rank on the upper left sleeve (see p. 65) were used to distinguish ranks. The starting point for the army's camouflage suits can be regarded as the triangular tent sections used by the Reichsheer since 1927, originally made of gray mako cotton, and covered in camouflage colors in June of 1936. The camouflage color pattern, with a light and a

The triangular tent section was an important piece of rain protection for the infantrymen and was part of the field equipment always to be carried by the man.

Winter and camouflage combat uniforms, as introduced in 1942-43 as auxiliary equipment.

dark side, was used until the end of World War II and was adopted by the Bundeswehr with slight variations.

The 1944 combat uniform was to be introduced as a standardized battle dress for all parts of the Wehrmacht. Its development originated from the availability of material at that time. The thriftiest use of material and the practical experience of war had to be kept in mind. Before the end of the war, troop testing of this uniform was carried out. A general introduction never took place.

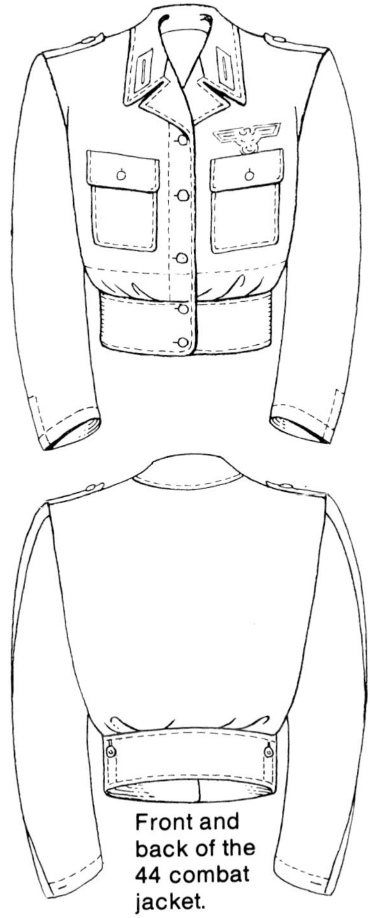

Front and back of the 44 combat jacket.

Combat uniform, 1944 model.

Bundeswehr Combat Uniforms

The uniforming of the Bundeswehr was done with the tradition of previous army uniforms consciously in mind. But one exception was the combat uniform in camouflage colors. The two-piece battle dress, composed of the jacket with its hood, the trousers with their suspenders, plus combat boots, an olive knit shirt, and a steel helmet, developed from experiments with combat dress made by the European Defense Community (EVG).

World War II experience gained with camouflaged clothing and equipment was also utilized. In the war the camouflaged jacket and trousers were not inherent parts of the uniform as they are in the Bundeswehr. The spot camouflage of the Bundeswehr combat suit was very reminiscent of the camouflage pattern of the triangular tent panels used by the Wehrmacht arms troops. Also part of the combat uniform was the two-ply steel helmet (a plastic helmet with a steel cover over it), as were the laced shoes with attached short leather leggings. This footgear included in

"Uniforms and Insignia of the Armed Forces"—with this title the Bundeswehr authorities published its first guide to the new military uniforms as of February 1, 1956. The camouflage pattern of the combat uniforms as pictured (above) did not correspond to reality (see photo at right). Only in July of 1959 did the first uniform regulations for Bundeswehr soldiers appear in ZDV 37/10.

A senior corporal in the camouflage combat uniform, the M1A1 helmet and camouflage net, and the rapid-fire 7.62 x 51 DM 1 (FN) rifle. At right beside him is a corporal in the work uniform with the work cap resembling the Wehrmacht's 43 field cap in cut. The camouflage pattern of the combat uniform (with angles) differed from that of the trapezoid tent panels (round). The senior corporal carries the rolled tent panel atop his assault kit.

the first outfitting did not work out well. For the infantrymen the half-height leather boots, also known as "dice cups", remained the ideal footgear. Their greatest handicap was the equation of Prussian-German militarism with the marching tread of these nailed boots. This unfortunate allusion alone discredited the boots as possible footgear for the Bundeswehr. But the hesitancy was not to last long. For the practical advantages were all too clear. After just a short time the combat boots were introduced, now with rubber soles without hobnails, and equipped with a clasp to narrow the circumference of the top. The work clothes of uniform olive green moleskin fabric was also complete only with half-height laced shoes and olive canvas leggings. This combination of footgear had proved to be practical midway through World War II and was to be retained by the Bundeswehr into the late Seventies.

This battle dress, weathertight and presumably protective against infrared viewing, was used for only a short time. On June 8, the third directive of the federal president said of the soldiers' uniforms: "3. The combat uniform is of one color." The greatest problem with the first combat uniform was its poor protection against cold-

ness. The combat jacket and trousers of solid-color "mottled hunting" wollen cloth were to solve this problem. This scratchy combat uniform, wearable only with long underwear, was immortalized in Infantry slang as the "felt louse." Meanwhile the mottled combat suit disappeared into the storehouses, and the work clothes advanced, with appropriate finishing touches in terms of cut and quality, to become a combat uniform or battle dress in the Seventies and Eighties. With this development there also came the equipping of the

Above: The first Bundeswehr soldiers were issued the American M1A1 helmet, composed of a steel cover painted NATO olive and a gray plastic helmet with a lining. Here the plastic helmet is shown, which was worn for parades, sentry duty and also maneuvers (left). At the request of the Allies, the Wehrmacht steel helmet was no longer used. Since German industry did not regard itself as capable of developing a new helmet model quickly, the choice had to be made in favor of the not very practical American model. In September of 1958 the new one-piece model FJ 60 steel helmet was introduced, followed in May of 1960 by the present-day model.

Left: How the plastic model was worn for light service in the field, here by a radioman. With his camouflage combat uniform he wears black laced leather shoes with attached leather leggings. This footgear did not prove practical and was replaced by half-height combat boots.

Far left: The expansive form of the steel bell of the M1A1 helmet can be seen clearly here. It appears to balance on the head only with difficulty.

The solid-color combat uniform of the Sixties was made of scratchy woolen cloth that won it the name of "felt louse."

armored grenadiers and pursuit troops with laced combat shoes, such as were originally worn only by paratroopers. The original concept for the infantry uniforms, comprising the combat uniform (camouflaged), work suit (olive), and dress/mess uniform (gray), had meanwhile reduced itself to olive and gray uniform pieces. As of 1989 a three-part system is again being attempted. For infantry warfare in our degrees of latitude, the Bundeswehr is receiving a new combat uniform of five-colored spot camouflage.

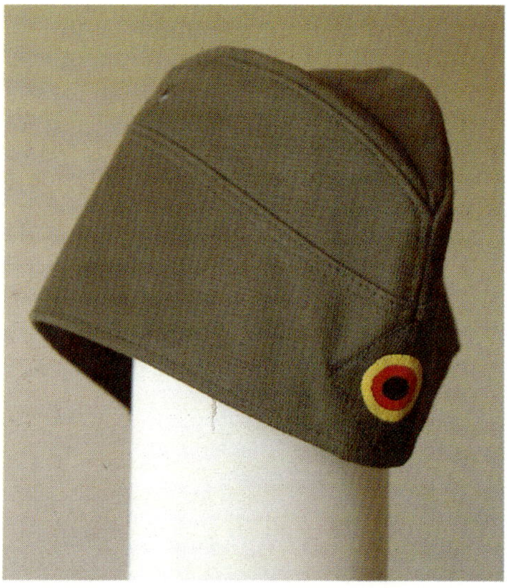

Since the Bundeswehr has been in existence, the "Schiffchen" cap of moleskin in NATO olive has been part of the infantryman's uniform. Only in the earliest years was an olive work cap, cut like the 43 field cap, worn. Before the "blessing" that allows the wearing of the beret, the young grenadiers of today must be content with this field cap.

Before the beret was introduced for all service arms in the early Eighties, only the newly formed pursuit units wore a green beret with golden oak leaves as their emblem (lower left). At first this beret emblem still had no national shield, such as the armored grenadiers had from the start (lower right). A service-color cord on the shoulder flap (above) served to indicate the service arm.

Left: A staff sergeant of the armored grenadiers in the combat uniform that was worn from the mid-Seventies until the introduction of the camouflaged uniform. Right: An armored grenadier in the work/combat uniform with sweater, which has been worn since 1980.

The "ground troop helmet" has been the standard steel helmet of the Bundeswehr since 1960; the lined version with neck strap is worn today. The rainwear (left) with overshoes, protective jacket and trousers has been introduced recently. Below: a winter field cap with peak plus ear and neck protection.

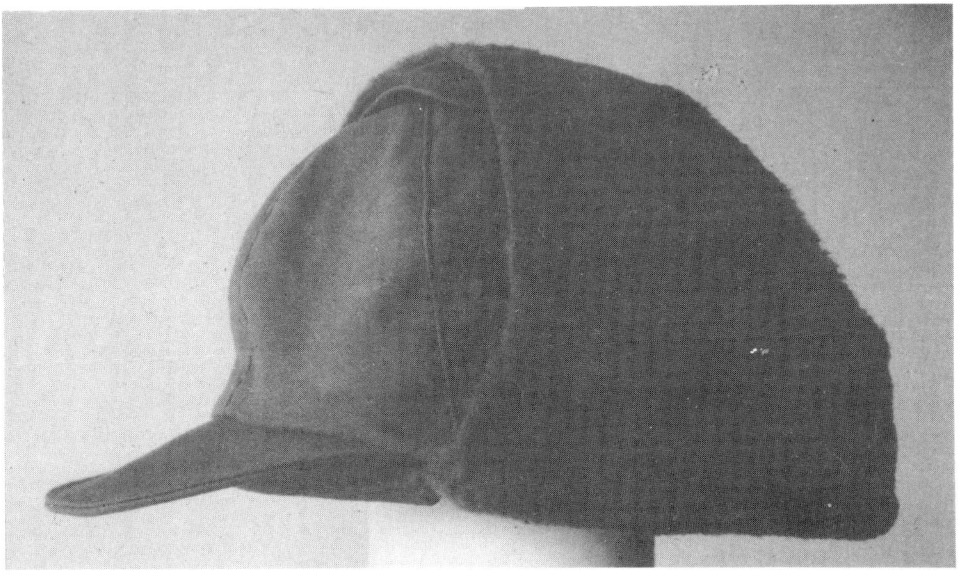

Until 1995, all Bundeswehr infantry troops are supposed to be equipped with the new spot camouflage uniform. The camouflage effect in comparison with the old combat uniform is easy to see below.

A New Start in Gray

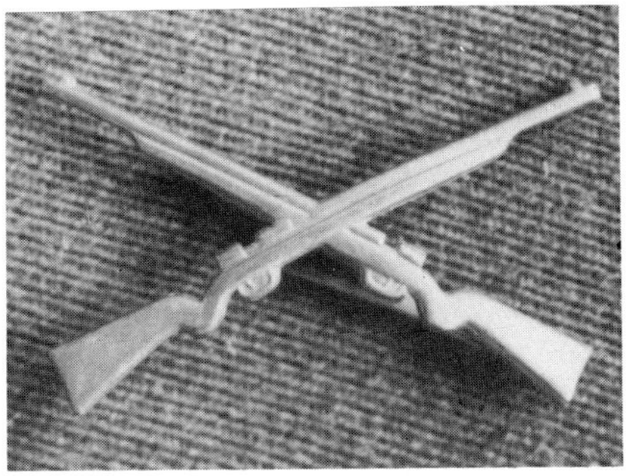

Before the reintroduction of service-color collar panels, service-arm emblems were worn on the collar corners of uniform jackets from November 1955 to December 1956. According to the planners' stylistic decisions, the infantry, the infantry's emblem was crossed rifles, which later reappeared as the armored grenadiers' beret emblem.

With the introduction of the new Bundeswehr uniform at the end of 1955, the three-part uniform system became visible: slate-gray dress/mess uniform, olive work uniform and camouflaged combat uniform. The choice of "slate gray" for the new uniforms and the almost complete lack of striking decorations, such as had "sparkled" on the Wehrmacht infantry uniforms, led to the judgment that this was a complete break with tradition. This is true of certain details such as insignia of rank on shoulder flaps, service-arm emblems or collar panels with patches of braid, and emblems on caps. But it is not so true of the cut of the slate-gray uniform jackets. For the dress

Woven enlisted men's collar panel.

uniform, a jacket with two rows of buttons and pointed conical shoulder flaps was introduced, which is also worn by non-commissioned officers and men as part of the mess uniform. The cut of this jacket is very reminiscent of the well-known tank jacket for the armored troops and assault artillery of World War II. Further similarities can also be found in the mess and dress jacket for officers and officer candidates. The second-class jacket for generals of the Luftwaffe from 1935 to 1945 can be regarded as the model for it. The new four-pocket jacket introduced in 1957, with its open collar and single row of buttons,

The gray service cap for officers looked like the 1943 field cap but lacked its practical aspects. The edge of the cap was not made to be folded down, and buttons had no function but decoration.

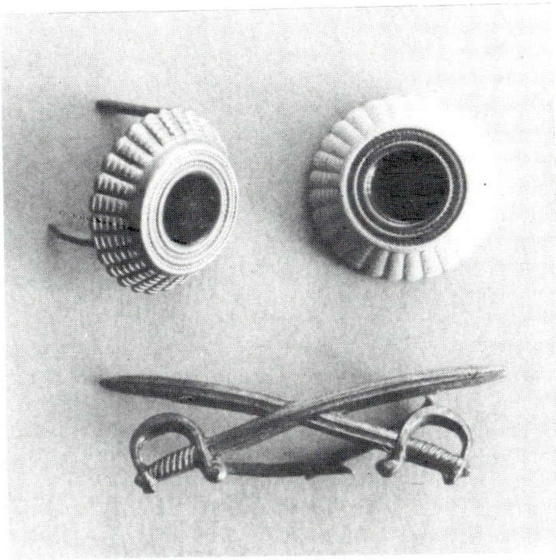

Above: Two different rosettes for the gray service cap and the non-commissioned officers' and men's peaked cap. At left is the first form with a matt, feltlike black eye. The rosette at right has a black painted eye. Under the rosettes is a pair of crossed sabers made of gold-colored metal, which was worn on the service cap and the olive armored corps beret.

Below: The peaked cap for non-commissioned officers and men had metal emblems as well as service-color piping. This is the emblem of the army section of the armed forces.

The first postwar headgear (from top to bottom): Peaked cap, gray for generals, with embroidered emblems. Service caps, gray for officers, with piping at the top, and for non-commissioned officers and men, with metal emblems; work cap, olive, with woven emblems,

made clear a relationship with the old Luftwaffe uniform worn until 1945.

After the first "citizens in uniform" had appeared on the scene, an extensive discussion about their uniforms began. As the public saw it, the mess uniform was the chief offender, because that was the one the public saw most often. The obviously low public opinion and certain noteworthy practical deficiencies led to changes in the uniform picture within two years.

Starting with a list of faults which they were given, the Federal Defense Ministry took the consequences and brought back the traditional collar patches on service-color panels instead of service-arm insignia. The infantry did not, though, get their white service-arm color back and had to be satisfied with "hunter's green." Armored grenadiers had "light green" collar panels, and those of the armored

Above: The slate-gray jacket of a chief sergeant-major, circa 1963. The jacket, which was worn without a belt as part of the dress and mess uniforms, has grained antique gold-colored buttons plus a cord of metallic thread in the same color on the edge of the collar.

Right: The short jacket for the dress uniform was worn with a belt by officers, as well as without a belt by non-commissioned officers and men, with the mess uniform. This is a major's jacket, with silver-colored officer's piping on the edge of the collar. The rather unbecoming jacket slid higher and higher, especially while sitting, giving the wearer a "tail wind", which gave the jacket the ironic name of "Queen Luise Jacket."

pursuit troops were "dark green." Today the infantry, composed of pursuit troops and armored grenadiers, wears green panels and berets. For a time, the armored pursuit troops were given the rose color of the armored troops. When the four-pocket jacket was introduced, the optics were improved by changing the basic color of the jacket to medium gray and the trousers to dark gray. So once again the army wore "two types of fabric." In time the medium gray of the jacket evolved into the light gray of today. Certain changes and completions were made in 1962. At that time the embroidery on the officers' caps were introduced, as were round shoulder flaps for all ranks. The use of colored unit insignia also took place. The uniform picture was changed

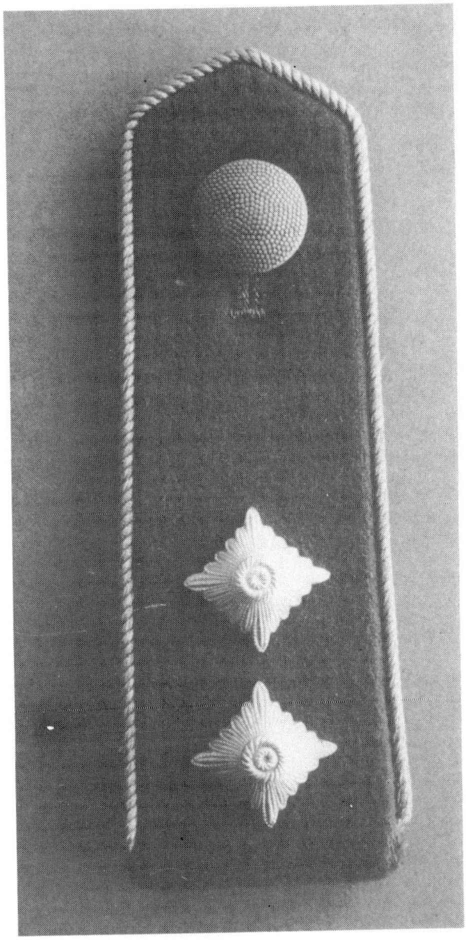

Above: The first type of shoulder flap with pointed top, for a first lieutenant. The flap has a silver-colored metal cord edging as well as chrome-colored metal stars. The flap, sewn on at the bottom, is held at the top by a grained antique gold-colored button.

Left: In 1962 the shoulder-flap points were rounded off and given a service-color background for officers. The other shoulder flaps were bordered in the service color. Here is a colonel, also recognizable by the oak-leaf embroidery on the peak of his cap.

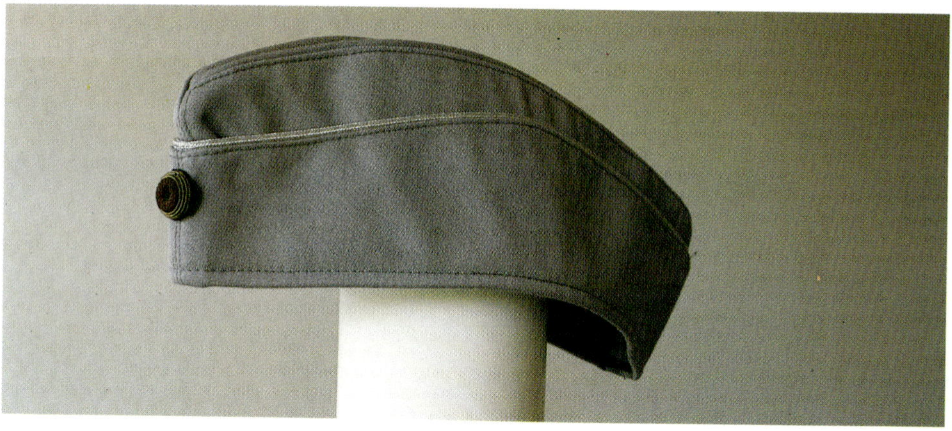

The year of 1962 brought many striking changes in Bundeswehr uniforms. For example, the gray service caps that resembled the 1943 field cap were replaced by a gray "Schiffchen" with the national rosette and appropriate piping. Non-commissioned officers and men wore this gray fore-and-aft cap with service-color piping on the folded-up sides. Oak-leaf embroidery was also introduced for staff officers, and band embroidery for lieutenants and captains, on the peak of the peaked cap. Officers basically wore embroidered emblems on their caps.

The medium gray four-pocket jacket with a single row of buttons, as worn by the infantry since 1957. This is the dress jacket of a lieutenant. The gray jacket was originally worn with dark gray trousers that had service-color pipings. Later the jackets became lighter and the trousers darker, tending toward black.

A staff sergeant (left) as a sergeant on duty (blue cord on the right shoulder), and a master sergeant, uniformed as of 1959. They both wear the dress uniform with an olive field belt. The black leather belt with antique silver-colored metal box buckle was introduced only in 1962.

An information brochure of 1970, used by the Bundeswehr in recruiting, presents these "dynamic" figures as examples of the various uniforms that include the gray uniform jacket. From left to right: Class A, dress and mess uniforms.

The lack of an appropriate uniform for social occasions led in 1963 to the introduction of the two-pocket jacket with silver-colored aiguilette. This is the jacket of a lieutenant colonel of the infantry. Since 1973 officers have worn a black dress jacket in the form of the mess jacket.

Infantry Insignia of Rank since March 1974

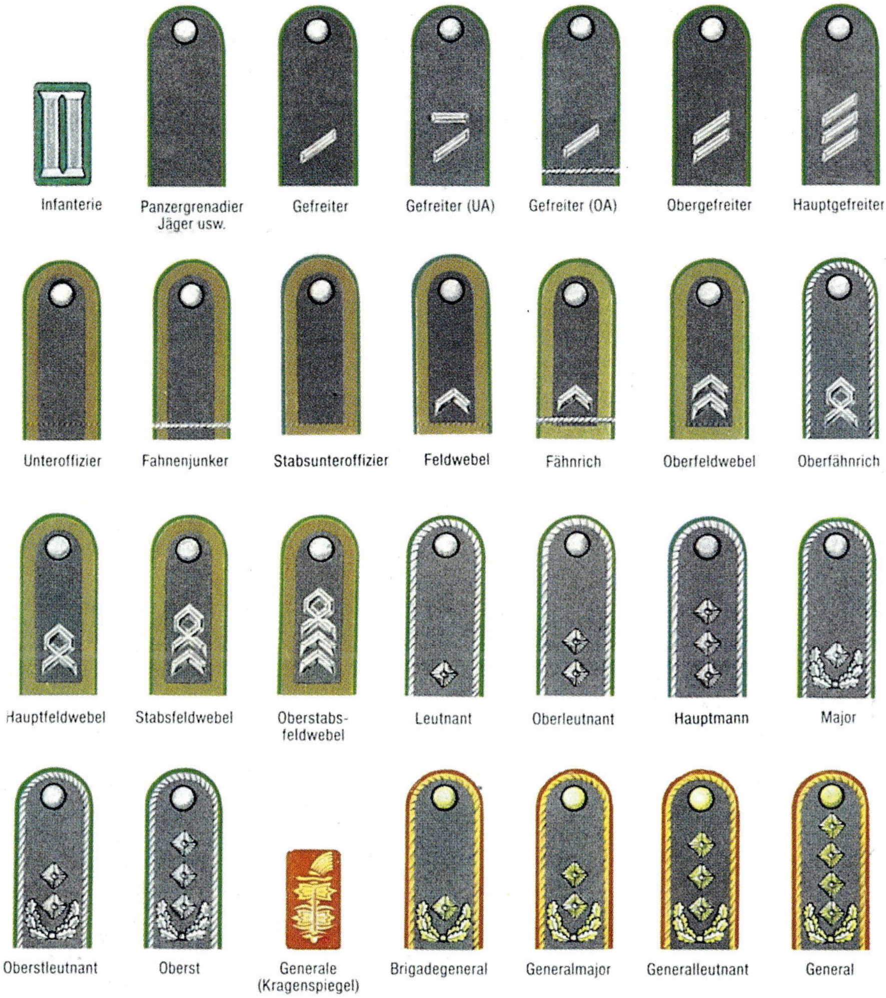

strikingly once again by the introduction of the beret, which replaced the peaked cap for non-commissioned officers and men. Officers still can choose between the two.

Insignia Without a Swastika

The July 26, 1957 law concerning titles, orders and medals allowed the wearing of old World War I and II medals on uniforms. In the fifth section of the law, the manner of wearing them was regulated: "(1) Orders and medals, as well as other insignia, that are to be worn as a ribbon, are worn as medal ribbons on the left breast side, from right to left in the following order: 1. Service medals of the Federal Republic of Germany, 2. Lifesaving medals on a ribbon, 3. Iron Cross of 1914, 4. Iron Cross of 1939, 5. Orders and medals for services in World War I, in order of awarding, 6. World War I cross of honor, 7. War service cross of 1939, 8. Other medals for service in World War II in order of awarding, 10. Governmentally approved models in order of awarding, 11. Foreign models in order of their class ranking." The medals that bore the national eagle of the Third Reich in their original condition must be "De-Nazified", which for those that held them meant a new manufacturing of the medals without swastikas. The manufacturers of

Above: Original-size medals, such as the "denazified" infantry assault emblem in silver shown here, can only be worn on the mess uniform or Class A uniform for special occasions.

Left: Prescribed manner of wearing small ribbons over the left breast pocket of the gray dress jacket.

Small medal ribbons of Major General Günther Vollmer, which could be worn on all occasions in this form on the gray jacket. From top to bottom and left to right are the following medals: Knight's Cross of the Iron Cross of 1939. Iron Cross First Class, Iron Cross Second Class, Close Combat Badge in bronze (bronze-colored miniature of the medal on a dark gray background), Wound Medal in silver, Infantry Assault Emblem in bronze and "Winter War in the East 1941/42" medal.

medals always produced these medals in their original size, or as miniatures for the medal ribbon or as pins. The opportunity of always bearing medals on the small medal ribbon was granted to the gray jacket.

Original-size medals, on the other hand, can only be worn on the mess uniform with permission.

The Close Combat Badge in silver in its original size, without national eagle and swastika.

Color on the Upper Arm

On November 27, 1962, when Federal President Heinrich Lübke approved the army unit emblems and let them be introduced, the soldiers of the 1st Mountain and 1st Air-landed divisions already were wearing their own cloth emblems on the upper left sleeves of their gray uniform jackets. The unit emblems of the army divisions with their heraldic symbols were to be worn by all divisions at their troop stations. In the opinion of the planners, the emblems would engender a positive feeling of belonging for all ranks. The "Division Corps Spirit" was thus to be given a connecting link. The schools, the Bundeswehr service offices and the home-guard commands also received their own insignia.

General Hansen, as Commander of the First Armored Division, wears the unit insignia of the former First Armored Grenadier Division. It shows the horse symbol of Lower Saxony on a background of yellow and white colors—a hint to the location of the division in and around Hannover.

Left: Unit emblems of the 6th Armored Grenadier Division with colored borders: Staff and division personnel silver-colored, first brigade white (here the 16th Armored Grenadier Brigade), second brigade red (here the 17th Armored Grenadier Brigade), and third brigade yellow (here the 18th Armored Grenadier Brigade).

—Text of page 86—

Excerpts from the Regulation Texts

a) Regulations on the establishment of the Close Combat Badge of November 25, 1942

As a visible sign of recognition of the soldier fighting man-to-man with bayonet and close-combat weapons, but at the same time as an inspiration to the highest fulfillment of duty, I create the Close Combat Badge.

The awarding of the Close Combat Badge is to take place according to strictly followed criteria. The appropriate superior officers are responsible for the strictest application of the criteria.

Führer's Headquarters, November 25, 1942
The Führer and Supreme Commander of the Army
Adolf Hitler

b) Criteria

to the order on the creation of the Close Combat Badge of November 25, 1942

1. The Close Combat Badge is awarded to recognize the soldier who had repeatedly done his duty appropriately in close "man-to-man" combat with his weapon in hand.

The Infantry Assault Medal remains independent thereof, along with the special conditions required to attain it.

2. The Close Combat Badge will be awarded on three levels and worn on the left side, 1 cm above the medal ribbon. When a higher level is won, the former one is to be removed. Nevertheless it remains in the holder's possession.

3. The criteria for awarding are:
For the 1st level (bronze) 15 close combats
For the 2nd level (silver) 30 close combats
For the 3rd level (gold) 50 close combats

4. To be counted as close combat days are:
a) All battle days in which the soldier to be honored had the opportunity to see "the whites of the enemy's eyes", that is, to fight against the enemy man-to-man with close-combat weapons to the final decision.
b) This can thus take place in a large attack, in scouting troop forays, in defensive action, in an individual report mission, in an enemy scouting troop action, etc.
c) The location—at a battle outpost, in the frontal field, in the main battle line, in the artillery firing position, in the rear army area (for example, in action against partisans) or in an attack on an ambulance train or a supply column—is of no importance.

5. Every soldier who comes into a situation as described under section 4 unprotected and on foot, and defends himself there, has eligibility for the badge.

6. a) At the suggestion of the company leader, who is to report promptly—on the same day, whenever possible—the commanders of the regiments, independent battalions, etc., are daily commanded to record the close combat days to be counted for the participating units.

7. Every soldier has a sheet to be carried in his salary book (Type 2), on which he is to record and substantiate the eligible close combat days.

For commanders, from company commanders up, the close combat day is to be attested to by the next higher superior officer involved in the action in question, who provides the applicable second documentation in the personal papers.

8. a) The close combat days are to be counted beginning with December 1, 1942.
b) In order to favor often-tested veteran front-line fighters, however, in cases of uninterrupted action in the East, 1) after June 22, 1941, 2)
in 15 months up to 15 close combat days
in 12 months up to 10 close combat days
in 8 months up to 5 close combat days
may be added after a careful examination of the records kept by the unit commander.
c) The division commander can award the Close Combat Badge to soldiers who, because of severe wounds, will have no future opportunity to take part in close combat. 3)

For this, the soldier must have proof as follows:
for the first level, at least 10 close combat days
for the second level, at least 20 close combat days
for the third level, at least 40 close combat days

As for the reckoning of close combat days before December 1, 1942, see section b).

9. a) For fallen, deceased and fatally wounded soldiers, the Close Combat Badge may be awarded posthumously if they fulfilled the criteria before their death or on the day of their death. The awarded badge is to be sent to their next of kin along with the certificate of possession as a memorial.
b) Soldiers taken prisoner or gone missing lose their eligibility for the Close Combat Badge.

10. The company or other commander empowers the awarding of the appropriate level of the Close Combat Badge by the appropriate regimental or battalion or section commander (Type 3,).

For the awarding of the Close Combat Badge, the certificate of possession (Type 4,) is to be filled out by the conferring commander. Only these certificates empower the wearing of the Close Combat Badge.

With the GERMAN UNIFORMS OF THE 20TH CENTURY series, a gap in the specialist literature is closed. The limitation to one service arm, yet with the time span from World War I to the present, is especially rewarding. The first volume includes, in words and pictures, the **Uniforms of the Panzer Troops.** The uniforms of the panzer troops are presented to the observer completely and thoroughly in many impressive pictures, usually hitherto unpublished, and precise descriptions.